Arts Resource Handbook

Arts Resource Handbook

Activities for Students with Disabilities by Paula Chan Bing

Project Overview by Kathleen Gaffney

A Joint Partnership of Arts Horizons, Inc. and Artsgenesis, Inc.

LIBRARIES
U N L I M I T E D
A Member of the Greenwood Publishing Group

Westport, Connecticut • London

LIBRARIES UNLIMITED
Teacher Ideas Press
A Member of Greenwood Publishing Group, Inc.
88 Post Road West
Westport, CT 06881
1-800-225-5800
www.lu.com

Library of Congress Cataloging-in-Publication Data

ISBN 1-59158-026-9

Contents

 # Acknowledgments

In 1992, Arts Horizons, Artsgenesis, and New York City's District 75/Citywide programs applied for and received a National Endowment for the Arts three-year arts grant for $150,000 for Project A.R.I.S.E. (Arts Resources in Special Education). In addition, the partnership engaged Anne Dennin, who very successfully raised another $500,000 from the private sector.

It initially seemed that this was more than sufficient funding for Project A.R.I.S.E. But over the course of the project, we learned that we would serve 57 schools with students having 11 different types of severe or multiple disabilities. Thanks to the project's artistic director, Kathleen Gaffney, staff development workshops for teachers and artists-in-residence workshops for students were modified, first for special education and then customized for these 11 specific populations.

Thanks also to the acting superintendent, Jack LaRock, who encouraged the NEA application and signed off on the proposal. And special thanks to Evie Silberman, arts coordinator of District 75 and project liaison to A.R.I.S.E. We could not have had the success we realized without her dedication and hard work. Thanks to Paula Bing for writing and compiling the activities for this book. Paula was one of our many superb and dedicated teaching artists who participated in this three-year project.

Most of all, thanks to the teachers and artists of Project A.R.I.S.E., who embraced the development workshops and used the techniques with the students. There were many successes in academic, social, and higher-order thinking development, to name a few.

One of our favorite anecdotes is about a class who could not focus long enough to participate in fire drills. It was through dance and movement activities that these students not only participated but looked forward to the drills. Through the work of the artist-in-residence in 1995, that teacher continues to use those arts activities today to help her students to realize their full potential.

John Devol, executive director, Arts Horizons
Roger Shea, executive director, Artsgenesis

Project Overview

A.R.I.S.E. Artistic Director Kathleen Gaffney

*An invasion of armies may be resisted, but not
an idea whose time has come.*

—Victor Hugo

For nearly four years, two arts-in-education organizations and one New York City school district focused their energy and substantial resources on a comprehensive project to help students with disabilities and special education teachers spontaneously extend their limits through the arts. This project was called A.R.I.S.E. (Arts Resources in Special Education). I was privileged to be the project's artistic director. My role was to design the artists-in-residence program serving 1,800 students; to train a highly experienced core of 32 artists; and to create and lead the three-year Saturday Teacher Institute, an intensive series of staff development experiences for the 95 participating teachers.

Project A.R.I.S.E. began in 1992 and was born as a result of a confluence of events involving these two arts organizations (Arts Horizons and Artsgenesis), a school district (District 75/Citywide Programs), and a government agency (the National Endowment for the Arts). Across the country, multiple intelligences (MI) theory was emerging as the most viable way to view the child as a whole. In those days, the theory maintained that human beings were intelligent in at least seven ways. MI's wide acceptance in the educational community allowed me to align our project with solid principles of human cognition. So, galvanized with the belief that all children can learn if they are approached through their core intelligences, we set about proving that the arts were the key to unlocking ability.

We launched the largest, most comprehensive arts-in-special-education plan conceived in the United States up to that time, just as the Goals 2000 and state and national standards were gathering momentum. Our goal of teaching academic subjects by integrating them with the arts now had to be crafted to meet those standards. Ours was a very ambitious and precise task.

This handbook reflects successful standards-compatible lessons, field-tested in special education classrooms during the span of Project A.R.I.S.E. The lessons have been compiled as the partners' legacy, to inspire ideas and detail activities for educators and parents. Those who understand that children with disabilities need alternative learning strategies will find themselves well partnered by the artists whose work is contained in these lessons. And this handbook exists because the project partners felt an urgent need to leave a legacy, a path for others to follow. What you hold here is the Project A.R.I.S.E. legacy.

We were blessed that all project partners came to A.R.I.S.E. with many years' experience in the field of arts-in-education and the belief that the arts—theater, dance, music, and the visual arts—can transform a child's life, and I had a personal mission driving me. My own child had been rescued from autism through the arts.

My daughter, Kerrianne, was perfectly normal at birth, but 11 months later she was diagnosed with cancer of the eye. Three weeks after her operation for retinoblastoma, she received an MMR shot (measles, mumps, and rubella). Within 24 hours she had contracted measles, then meningitis, which led to profound neurological damage. My husband and I consulted many specialists, but our baby was pronounced autistic and severely developmentally disabled. At this juncture, I discovered early intervention and enrolled my daughter in three very innovative programs that required one of the parents to attend school with the child every day. We attended school together five days per week for two years.

Kerrianne and I worked with physical therapists, occupational therapists, and pediatricians of every ilk; developmental psychologists; cognitive specialists; and my true heroes in life, special educators. Our daughter's remarkable story has been told on CBS and PBS television programs, has been featured in *The New York Times,* and is the subject of a book, *Exceptional Path,* so its place in this chronicle is simply to show that a child began to emerge from autism as the result of music therapy. I called it a miracle. The developmental psychologist called it "spontaneously extending her limits." I witnessed the arts—music and visual arts, theater, and dance—miraculously reclaiming her mind and spirit. I wanted to understand how and was led to Dr. Howard Gardner's book, *Frames of Mind: The Theory of Multiple Intelligences* (Basic Books, 1983) and brain-based research.

Kerrianne Gaffney Shea, the child who "recovered" from autism as a result of music therapy. She learned everything through the arts. The ability to "spontaneously extend limits," became the driving force behind Project A.R.I.S.E. Courtesy of Phototake, Inc.

In this time when we as a nation are discovering the new meaning of *hero,* let me say that special education teachers are true heroes. I have seen many of them in action and stood in awe at their boundless energy, laser beam intention, and what seemed to me deep wells of patience. Their jobs are incredibly challenging, frustrating, heart breaking, and occasionally rewarding. Yet they are driven by an inner mission. For many of us in the field of education, the teaching we do today might not show up in front of us. This is triply so for special educators. In many lives they make all the difference in a child's ability to learn, and they need more tools, more ideas, new methods.

To understand how the activities in this book stimulate learning, we must first examine the theory and exactly how the arts fit like a hand in that MI glove. For some children with severe disabilities the arts are not only the best way to learn new material, they are the only way.

A Brief Journey into Multiple Intelligences Theory

To understand MI theory and its arts applications, let's begin with a very basic overview of the concept of human cognition. Until 1983, it was believed that human intelligence was fixed at birth, a result of heredity, and that nothing much could affect the given amount a person had. If intelligence was a blob of clay, you could fashion your clay into specific shapes. Even if you had the same amount as someone else, the result might "look" different. One fact was indisputable: that was all the clay you had to work with; you couldn't get any more. For decades, the assumption was that if it was true that the amount of intelligence you had was fixed at birth, then it could be measured in your childhood. This measurement could be used to predict how well you would succeed. This idea was furthered at the turn of the twentieth century by the work of Alfred Binet, a Frenchman who conceived of a test for intelligence. Intelligence testing swept across America and permeated every area of life, from the military to business and industry. No discipline embraced testing with more relish than education. Here was an instrument that could measure progress and probable success. But there was one slight problem: These tests might measure how well a student would do in school, but they failed to predict how well that child would do in life. And so the stage was set for the volcanic effect of the work of Dr. Howard Gardner. Dr. Gardner and his colleagues found that human beings were intelligent in at least 7 (now 9) ways. If we could assess a child's core intelligences, educators could use those strengths to help that child learn in areas that were less developed. There are a few specifics to keep in mind about MI theory.

All human beings possess all the intelligences. We all have all of them. What makes each human being unique is the way in which the intelligences work together in each of us. Remarkably, even if there is no clear path to that intelligence, an individual may possess it in abundance. Helen Keller, who could not hear or see, had a great deal of linguistic intelligence but no clear pathway to develop it until her gifted teacher, Anne Sullivan, found a bodily kinesthetic pathway. Ms. Sullivan placed the finger spelling shape for W in Helen's hand and placed her other hand in water. The message was clear: The hand sign stood for water. Then, like a key going into a lock and all the tumblers moving, Helen began to understand that these hand shapes stood for things, then eventually for ideas.

Most people have the ability to develop each intelligence to a higher level. Even if we are 106 years old we can still learn something new, still develop undeveloped intelligence. Neurologists tell us that the act of learning keeps our brains young. A key project component was to leave the teachers with the ability to integrate the arts after the project was completed. The Saturday Institute gave teachers the opportunity and instruction to develop the artist in themselves.

The intelligences are always interacting with each other in complex ways. Let us use the example of a young lady who plays the trumpet. The act of playing requires musical intelligence and also bodily kinesthetic intelligence to breathe properly and coordinate her fingers on the valves. She must also have interpersonal intelligence to follow the subtle signals of the conductor and be constantly aware of what the musicians around her are doing. If the performance requires an improvised solo, she must rely on her intrapersonal intelligence to capture her ideas and feelings in sound.

There are many ways to be intelligent within each area. Using another musical example, there is a young man who does not like to sing or play an instrument, but he relies on his musical intelligence for information. He places his ear to the ground so that he can predict how many buffalo there are, in which direction they are moving, and how quickly they might arrive. He does all this by interpreting sound vibrations. This is another manifestation of musical intelligence. Many children with disabilities manifest ability in intelligences other than linguistic and logical–mathematical.

The Intelligences

Do not think that my elementary descriptions begin to capture the scope or complexity of this groundbreaking concept. My intention is to provoke educators and parents to view human intelligence differently and to recommend that each artist conduct a further and more in-depth study.

Linguistic Intelligence

Linguistic intelligence is the ability to use words or symbols that stand for words to convey meaning. Our Western culture is dominated by the written and spoken word. Politicians and lawyers must develop this intelligence. If we look at linguistic intelligence and apply Gardner's criteria, we know it has a symbol system, the alphabet. Almost every culture including the deaf culture has a symbol system for words or sounds. From the beginning of time human beings have sought to form a way to express their thoughts and feelings to communicate. To the deaf culture it is sign language and finger spelling. Goods and services are certainly made from linguistic intelligence. From newspapers to plays to novels to the owner's manual in your car, ideas are most often transmitted via language, spoken or written. Is there value in our culture for the written or spoken word? Walk into a library or a bookstore, listen to a newscast, or spend time in nearly any classroom in America. The major transmission of knowledge in this country's classrooms is through language. Hopefully, the language the teacher is using is one students understand.

A high manifestation of linguistic intelligence occurs in someone like a journalist, a novelist, or a playwright who manipulates syntax and meaning. A perfect example of someone with a vast amount of linguistic intelligence is a poet. A poet can take just a few words and infuse them with incredible meaning by placing them in a certain order.

Logical–Mathematical Intelligence

Logical–mathematical intelligence is the ability to count, compare, calculate, and classify to understand the world around us. It is highly valued in our country, and much of our progress in the twentieth century came as a result of ideas and products from science, engineering, and economics, all requiring logical–mathematical thinking. Interestingly, this intelligence requires creativity to produce invention. It has become the dominant god in our modern constellation, the rationale for life, as well as the goal. And why not? What else has been able to deliver so much power into our hands?

Logical–mathematical intelligence is certainly powerful, valuable, and responsible for improving the conditions under which we live. It has aided us immeasurably in our capacity to survive. It has given us vaccines, larger tomatoes, the Dow Jones Industrial Average, television, cellular phones, computers, video games, our walk on the moon, Teflon, the microwave oven, the Internet, and the ability to obliterate the planet with the flick of a switch. With logical–mathematical intelligence delivering the power of life and death into our hands, our culture has begun to trust only the information we obtain from this intelligence. Please do not misunderstand: I am terribly grateful that I live in a time when ultrasound can show a fetus moving inside a woman's body. I am thankful that certain cancers can be cured. Medical science cured my own baby of cancer, but I sometimes feel the pendulum has swung too far.

Musical Intelligence

Musical intelligence is the ability to understand the world through sound and experience ease in identifying sound patterns, including various environmental sounds. People with this intelligence may hear tones or rhythms in their heads and often become composers. Morse code uses musical intelligence, as do sonar and ultrasound. When we can identify family members by listening to their footfalls we are using this intelligence. Research shows that musical intelligence actually develops logical–mathematical intelligence. Often, people with the latter intelligence become the most avid music lovers, collectors, record producers, and disc jockeys. Musical intelligence is not strictly limited to a narrow definition but encompasses other interpreters of sounds such as doctors. The doctor who first developed the stethoscope was a flutist.

Cosmologists zeroed in on the Big Bang by listening to the traces of sound that can still be heard from that cataclysmic event. Music is used in our ceremonies; in spiritual worship; and when we court, marry, and die. Music has been found to be the most direct way to change our emotional states. Musicians say it is because we all have a heartbeat within us.

Bodily–Kinesthetic Intelligence

Bodily–kinesthetic intelligence deals with physical movement and the knowledge of the body and how it operates. People who possess this intelligence develop a keen mastery over the motions of their bodies, (dancers, athletes) or are able to manipulate objects with finesse (ballplayers, surgeons, instrumentalists). This also includes those to whom the use of the body is central, such as surgeons or physical therapists. This intelligence entails the ability to understand the world through the body, to express ideas and feelings, and actually to communicate to others physically. We see this intelligence in children who cannot sit still for long, those who are well coordinated, and those who need to touch things to learn.

Visual–Spatial Intelligence

Central to this intelligence is the ability to perceive the visual world accurately and in three dimensions. Individuals who exhibit this intelligence are architects, navigators, cosmologists, sculptors, visual artists, filmmakers, choreographers, set designers, and chess players. This intelligence involves the ability to understand, perceive, internalize, and transform space. A choreographer must possess it to create patterns in space using human bodies. A coach needs it to diagram plays. A topographer, a bridge builder, and a cosmologist who charts the heavens must have it also. Visual artists who can represent form, contrast, line, shape, and color use this intelligence when they create.

People who have this intelligence often enjoy chess, like many colors, do jigsaw puzzles, and can imagine the world from a bird's eye view. They are best taught using pictures or photographs or by asking them to draw their ideas. When I walk into a classroom I can tell immediately if the teacher uses his or her spatial intelligence. There will be artwork everywhere. The desks will be on a diagonal. There will be mobiles hanging and bright colors evident.

Interpersonal Intelligence

This intelligence governs our relationships with others. It is the ability to notice and make distinctions in other people's moods and feelings. When we inspire others or have compassion for or empathy with them, we are employing interpersonal intelligence. Some of those who possess it are religious leaders, skilled teachers, parents, therapists and counselors, coaches, and directors. Business leaders point to interpersonal intelligence as essential in their work force. The performing arts—theater, dance, and music (where students are working together as a group)—develop it.

This intelligence consists of the ability to understand, perceive, and discriminate among people's moods, feelings, motives, and intentions. In artists it is the ability to "read" their audiences, modulate their feelings, bring them to tears, make them laugh, and provide them with insight into their lives. The artist must be an expert in the human terrain and "hold a mirror" to humanity.

Teachers are interpersonally intelligent. This is probably what drew them into teaching. After several weeks with a class they are able to take the emotional temperature of every child simply by walking into the room. This intelligence serves us in our relationships as well. It is our rudder; it is our gauge. How am I doing? Can I ask for the raise today? Do they love me? Are they angry? Will we break up? A child with disabilities is often deficient in this intelligence. The performing arts develop and hone it.

Intrapersonal Intelligence

This is the ability to have a relationship with ourselves. It involves access to our own feelings and emotions and the ability to tap inner resources. Words like *discipline, independent will, perseverance,* and *imagination* all help define this territory. A great man once said, "Everything in this world is created twice, first in our vision then in reality." This intelligence is responsible for creating that inner vision. Any art form will help develop this intelligence because they all require it. Intrapersonal intelligence involves the ability to know the self, to have an accurate reading of one's own internal landscape. Those who are strong in this intelligence can delay their own gratification. They can discipline themselves to finish a book, run a marathon, or stop fighting with a spouse.

I feel that this is the area in which our children experience the greatest deficit. They can't delay their own gratification. So many children lack impulse control. They do not seem to have any internal resources. We see the beginning of intrapersonal intelligence in a person who makes a list: not a list that reads buy milk, buy bread, but one that reads publish the book, make up with my mother, finish my degree. This second list is intended to motivate. Another early sign is when a child is content to play or study alone, can learn from failure, and can accurately express how he or she is feeling.

Naturalist Intelligence

This is the ability to understand, classify, and interpret the natural world and environment. Farmers, veterinarians, vintners, and great chefs use this intelligence in their work, as do individuals such as Charles Darwin, Jacques Cousteau, and Jane Goodall. Archeologists who read physical evidence of the past through preserved bones, meteorologists who read and predict weather systems, storm chasers, anglers, and scouts all must read the environment for clues and signs to function. Often we find excellent programs that use dolphins or horses in therapy with children who have disabilities. The children are responding with their natural intelligence.

Existential Intelligence

This is the need to pursue answers to the big questions. "Why are we here?" "Does the life of one person make any difference?" "What is a moral decision?" Humans have structured systems to grapple with these questions such as philosophy, religions, and codes of behavior. Dr. Gardner is still refining the details of this intelligence, but artists instinctively chart this intelligence with their work as they examine the meaning of life, war, death, and love with theater, dance, poetry, music, painting, and sculpture.

We hope this handbook will aid you in your work, give you many new ideas, refresh some older valued ones, inspire you, and assist you in carrying out your enterprise with children and the arts. In addition to teaching our children the ABCs, multiplication tables, and the noble gases, we must give them the tools with which to decode human experience. A well-known East Indian story goes like this: A poor man was begging in the street, claiming he was starving. And he was starving. A wealthy man was touched by the beggar's plight and gave him two coins, telling him to buy some bread. The wealthy man hid to watch the beggar. The beggar took one coin and bought a piece of bread. With the other coin he bought a flower. He placed the flower on the ground and sat looking at it as he ate his bread. The wealthy man, incensed that the beggar spent half the money on a flower, began to chastise him for his foolishness: "You could have bought a larger piece of bread with the other coin. Why did you waste it on a flower?" The beggar replied simply: "I did not waste it. Eating this bread allows me to live. Looking at this flower gives me the reason for living."

We hope you enjoy our flower.

Kathleen Gaffney, A.R.I.S.E. artistic director, designed the artist residencies, trained the artists, and created and conducted professional development for the 90 special educators. Courtesy of Kathleen Gaffney.

The Power of the Arts

 **George**

George had been sulking and crying all day. His face was frozen in a frightening frown, his brow wrinkled up, his eyes cast down, his lips thrust out in an enormous pout.

"Music—humph!" snorted George. "I ain't even lookin' up." The other nine-year-olds watched and waited until the artist-teacher finally pulled out a cassette tape.

"There's a fugitive on the loose," she said. "And you are the sound sheriffs who must find him. He's a fugitive theme in a fugue by Bach. And every time you hear him, he comes back disguised. You have to listen with your ears, not look with your eyes. He might return as a trumpet, a French horn, or even a trombone and tuba together. A 'sound disguise,' you might say. If you raise your hand every time he comes back, you'll get a badge. You'll graduate from Sound Sheriff School. But first you must catch him, every single time. Be careful, this fugitive theme is no fool!"

The music came on and students' voices were mute. They had already clapped the theme and heard it played on a flute. Hakim had even sung it, surprising everyone. But when the actual Bach theme was heard, excitement caused 12 hands to shoot up, waving like the wings of birds. George awakened as if from a dream. Even though he couldn't sing it, he too raised his hand every time he heard the theme.

The triumph of the sound sheriffs electrified the room. The excitement of the chase burned away the morning gloom. And when the theme had pounded out its final disguise, George jumped to his feet. He had fire in his eyes.

"I love that music! I LOVE that music! I want to hear it again! I want to take it home! Can I, can I, CAN I PLEASE?!"

But the artist couldn't answer. This was only visit number three. Tears would not be suitable for the students to see. She took a deep breath and wondered how many lovers of Bach there were who would never know his music. How many could never take Bach home?

George had been transformed. His body was straight. His eyes burned like coals and his hands gripped the desk.

"I guess I could make do with one less tape," she thought, and caught George's eyes as he smiled and wondered, "Now, why is that teacher crying?"

 The Transformative Power of the Arts

George is a child on Manhattan's Upper East Side. No one can know if George's musical experience stayed with him or disappeared forever, or if some day he will go out and buy his own CD of Bach fugues. Hearing Bach that day didn't help George learn to count, use proper English, or coordinate his movements. But for a moment, from somewhere deep inside himself, George found something that connected in a very unexpected way with something he never could have imagined. A very simple but profound thing had happened: George had heard music and was transformed.

George is one of a diverse group of students with special needs who are physically and mentally functional but lack emotional control and/or have attention deficit hyperactivity disorder. For these and other such children, the arts can be true lifesavers.

Because of the wide range of challenges faced by children with disabilities, it is understandable that developing physical, emotional, and psychological growth, as well as fulfilling required educational objectives, must be a teacher's primary concern. The arts not only provide "quality of life experiences" for severely challenged and lower functioning children but also stimulate and motivate both teachers and students. For those of you who have students like George, it is important to understand that art can tap a deep positive response that gives them a powerful motivation for constructively channeling their excessive and often explosive energy. Even if you are often overwhelmed by a multiplicity of practical concerns, it is vital to know who these particular children are and challenge both them and yourself with exposure to the power that the process of creating, experiencing, and perceiving the arts can unleash.

These are children who, despite their clinical classification, may have an "artistic temperament." This term is normally applied to the stereotypical, temperamental artist who flies into rages or ecstasies and then compulsively expresses this emotional energy as a dance, a piece of music, a play, or a painting. Beethoven, Edgar Allan Poe, Miles Davis, William Burroughs, and any number of people whom we call artistic geniuses could easily have been one of these children. Without art, their lives and their legacies would have been quite different.

Students with disabilities may be extremely sensitive, reacting and responding with great intensity of feeling to all stimuli. It is this intense emotional experience that demands some kind of outlet. These children may be like artists without an art form, and it is these same children who often have hidden talents in the arts. Yet we will never be aware of their gifts unless they are given the freedom to move or use a paintbrush, pen, or musical instrument.

For these children and others, be they physically, emotionally, intellectually, or otherwise disabled, the joys of release and expression through the arts can be life changing. Even if your first impulse is to assume that because a child is out of control, working in the arts would amplify that chaos, try taking the risk. You are likely to find it incredibly gratifying.

Arts Resource Handbook

Project A.R.I.S.E. (Arts Resources in Special Education) was the result of a joint partnership among Arts Horizons, Inc., Artsgenesis, Inc., and the National Endowment for the Arts in cooperation with New York City's District 75/Citywide Program. It was the largest arts-in-special-education project ever attempted in the United States. The project had many components: performances, a three-year series of intensive staff development, and artists-in-residence. This handbook focuses on the in-classroom arts activities in each of the art forms.

A.R.I.S.E. was funded by a cooperative agreement with the National Endowment for the Arts and the following:

New York City—District 75/Citywide

New York Telephone

Primerica/Travelers

American Express

Charles E. Culpepper Foundation

William and Mary Greve Foundation

New York City Department of Cultural Affairs

American Chai

Barker Welfare Foundation

Hyde and Watson Foundation

Morgan Stanley Foundation

Bell Atlantic Foundation

Project leaders who played a major role in this three-year project and teaching artists who contributed ideas and activities to this book include the following:

Project Leaders

John Devol, executive director, Arts Horizons, Inc.

Kathleen Gaffney, project artistic director and president, Artsgenesis, Inc.

Roger Shea, executive director, Artsgenesis, Inc.

Evie Silberman, arts coordinator, New York City District 75

Teaching Artists

Holly Fairbank, dance

Cheryl Hulteen, theater

Virginia Lockwood, music

Jan MacDougall, visual arts

Navida Stein, creative drama

Trudy Silver, music

# About the Handbook

This handbook was created to provide ideas about how the arts can be used across the curriculum and to develop multiple intelligences. Often, the goals in other areas of learning can supersede the art form. But the more you understand about the area of the arts with which you are working, the better you will be able to achieve your objectives. This handbook gives you simple steps and insight into the why, what, and how of adapting the arts to suit your situation.

Some Practical Suggestions

When you find an activity that appeals to you,

1. Read through the activity and any information about the art form.

2. See how participatory requirements fit your students' abilities. Make any necessary adaptations.

3. Look at what the activity can accomplish. Does this work for you, or can you change it slightly to better suit your objectives?

4. Look at the process and see which works best: working one-on-one or in a group, standing or sitting, and so forth. What modifications are best for your students?

5. In as little as 5 to 15 minutes, you can practice gestures, movements, sound-making, or other activities you may need to model for the students. Use a mirror if necessary. Although the time spent doing this can be brief, the clarity and security you bring to the classroom will be greatly increased.

6. Listen to the music at home before using it in class (this can actually be fun and relaxing).

7. Go over the sequence of steps in the activity. After you understand them, it will be easier to adapt them to your students as necessary.

8. Write a skeletal version of each step for yourself on an index card. Refer to this card as you lead your arts activity.

Does this sound like a lot of trouble? Perhaps. Is it worth it? Definitely. Does everyone have to do it? No. Working with the arts without the aid of an arts specialist is challenging and can be bewildering at first. The time you do commit to preparation will help you visualize the activity process so that you are not just following directions but understanding why you are doing what you do. The 30 minutes to an hour that you spend preparing can make a world of difference, and after your first time, it will be less and less necessary.

Process or Product?

In a written survey, teachers of children with special needs were asked which they thought was more important in an arts activity, the *process* of doing it, or the actual *product*. The majority of teachers spoke out for the importance of the process. Teachers of higher functioning students agreed that having a product, be it a poem, a work of art, or a performance, could provide a satisfying and dynamic closure to a series of arts experiences. Product-oriented arts activities can be a strong testimony to accomplishment and encourage feelings of self-esteem and confidence.

In visual arts, a product is almost inevitable. In the performing arts—dance, music, and drama—the process itself is a vital learning experience in creating, doing, and perceiving. As one teacher of autistic students expressed it, "Don't underestimate the value of quality of life experience that even a beautiful moment has for one of my kids." Remember, your product, although optional, can also be a "work-in-progress." This lets everyone, participants and observers alike, enjoy the outcome without feeling pressure.

Feel free to modify any of the activities in this handbook to emphasize process or stress product. Before making your choice (which could very well change midstream), assess the capabilities of your students as well as the time you are willing and able to commit, not just in time per session but in time that might stretch over a period of weeks, should that be necessary.

There is one point that is less difficult to understand if you have already experienced it. However familiar these students are with failure, they are probably even less well acquainted with success. Underestimating a student's abilities and lowering your sights could, in some cases, deprive that child of an opportunity to experience a very special success in working with the arts. Once in a while, consider taking a risk and challenging your students. Your own positive attitude and enthusiasm will greatly influence that of your students. Also, your own understanding of how to present an activity can strongly affect both the clarity of the process and any resulting product.

Consider the following if you are working primarily with *process*:

1. Stress the successes along the way on each given day.

2. Reflect back and evaluate the activity with your students, not judgmentally, but in terms of what was experienced. Don't just reinforce what was learned, give students a chance to consider what they liked or didn't and how they might change things next time. This reflection addresses the Workplace Readiness Standards.

Consider the following if you are working with a *product* or *performance*:

1. Be conscious of the timeline in planning for a culmination date. Sketch out what you would like to have accomplished in each session. You might even start with the last day first.

2. Allow *more* time to practice and rehearse than you think you'll need.

3. *Product* works best with activities that may develop over longer periods of time or when you have an artist-in-residence.

# Warm-Ups

It is no coincidence that athletes, dancers, musicians, and actors are all familiar with the benefits of warm-up. When musicians warm up, it is not just to loosen up their muscles; it is also to make the molecules of their instruments begin to vibrate at a faster speed so there will be an optimal clarity of response in their instruments when it is time to perform. If the body, the emotions, the psyche, and the intellect are the instruments through which we perform and participate, these too must be "warmed up" for maximum response, whether in the arts or in an athletic competition.

Like all of us, students with disabilities need a little transition time to move from one state of being to another. The arts are truly re-creational. Through them, we transform thoughts, feelings, and perceptions into color, shape, movement, and sound. Your students' fears of the unknown will transform into curiosity and enthusiasm when you ease them into this new land of multisensory experience with sensitive and creative preparations and warm-ups.

One way you can warm up your students for an arts activity is to introduce ideas related to some aspect of the main activity. If the main activity involves African dance, you could begin by introducing ideas and information about African culture or geography. You might show photos or pictures, listen to music, or read an African folktale.

Another type of warm-up is a group activity that incorporates some aspect of the upcoming arts activity. For example, if you are going to be doing "twig painting," you may want to take a nature walk. The nature walk need not be revealed as a prelude to an arts project; it can just be a walk outside during which students collect twigs. Or everyone can know ahead of time that they will be painting with twigs and will need to collect them for that reason.

The third type of warm-up draws students into active involvement with some element of the upcoming arts activity, but in a nonthreatening way. Such warm-ups can be gamelike and fun. You will find a number of "game warm-ups" in the activities sections of this handbook.

 Reflection

When an arts activity has ended, it does not have to mean the experience is over. Because creative moments are so fleeting, it is valuable to look again and re-share your experiences. Talk about specific reasons why John's mask looks scary or Awilda's puppet has a personality. Ask questions such as "Do you like what you did?" "What do you know now that you didn't know before?" "How did you feel when you started moving to the music?" "How do you feel now?" Some students may say they were scared about trying something new. Some may want to repeat a music or drama experience.

Reflection and repetition can prolong and amplify the original experience. As well as being a practical review of what has been learned, it helps clarify the experience of being in touch with one's own emotions and responses. Recent studies have shown that any experience, when linked simultaneously to powerful emotion, becomes strongly entrenched in the memory. This same effect occurs when learning is linked to bodily kinesthetic intelligence. The emotional and physical experiences your children have in their arts activities are the sun and rain that nurture the growth of all their intelligences. Reflection and repetition can keep those emotions alive beyond the original experience.

The recent trend of student portfolios and journals could be modified to your students' abilities. Collections of drawings and photos, or a shoebox filled with paint-covered twigs, red ribbons from a dance activity, or other memorabilia can be powerful reflection tools in stimulating memories and emotions relating to the arts experience.

For yourself, reflection can help you assess your own successes and failures. Writing notes and thoughts in an arts activities journal can let you record ideas for improvement, memorable moments, and what you have learned from your students in the rich and challenging processes you have shared together.

CHAPTER ONE

Dance and Movement

When they give themselves up, they clap their hands; When they leave behind the imperfections of self, they dance.

—Jalludin Rumi, Persian poet, twelfth century, *The Mathnavi*

The Dance of Life: An Introduction

Dance celebrates the movement of the body through time and space. By experiencing the joy of movement, we connect with the rhythms inside us and the space outside us. There is a natural link between dance and our life experiences. As with dance, our life movements involve reacting to, and interacting with, all aspects of our environment and those within it. Dance, with its raw element of movement, can transcend language and other cultural differences to communicate powerfully on a universal level. A leap for joy or a cry of sadness are spontaneous expressions of human emotions in their most natural forms.

Movement in dance has differing qualities of energy. It can create many gestures and shapes. There are pathways to follow on the ground and different levels to explore in space. As with melodies, rhythms, or visual designs, movement can imitate, repeat, and create patterns. Movement can contrast opposites: high and low levels in space, big and small gestures, weak and strong energies, and fast and slow modes of locomotion (ways of traveling through space). A person can move alone or with others. Dance can be wild and improvised, careful and planned, or use a combination of both approaches. In its total cessation, movement becomes utter stillness.

We are more familiar than we think with all the aspects of how we move our bodies. Movement is something we experience in the dance of our own lives, from birth to death. Our bodies, the space around them, and the energy or force with which we propel ourselves through time and space all relate back to our first movements inside our mothers' wombs.

Adapting Movement Activities to Diverse Populations

Movement is an affirmation of life. For children with disabilities, there is much that is beyond their control. Controlling one's body can be a metaphor for controlling one's life, and just as important, for *wanting* to control one's life.

1

The movement activities in this chapter are appropriate for a wide range of students with disabilities. Some have been designed especially for severely disabled children. Others address higher functioning students. In their full form, they may be too complex for some children, yet children with disabilities need to get their bodies moving. If creating a dance is beyond your students' abilities, take the seeds of these movement ideas and adapt them. A seed does not have to blossom into a tree to be of value.

Movement has the benefit of improving circulation, muscle tone, and neuromuscular coordination. Children who use wheelchairs can, with help, enjoy the sensations of fast and slow or paths that zigzag, curve, and spiral—something they might rarely experience. Children who are autistic or those with speech challenges can find a wonderful release of pent-up tension and emotion. Others can watch movements that create patterns and change shapes in space. Children who are hearing impaired or deaf can feel vibrations on the floor, in stereo speakers, or on light rubber balls or balloons.

The information, definitions, and details about dance and movement in this section are for your own enrichment, understanding, and reference. Do not feel you have to use them in every activity. Be bold in your adaptations and trust your knowledge of your students. Do not be afraid of utter simplicity. These activities are only the basic recipe; your creativity is the secret ingredient.

What Makes a Dance?

Like a story, play, or piece of music, a dance has a beginning, a middle, and an end. A dance contains movement ideas or patterns of movement ideas that can be arranged into a form.

Form in Dance

Form in any arts discipline is simply a "shape" that results from a plan of how to organize the ideas. Choreographers of dances (like composers of music) often give these ideas names such as **A**, **B**, or **C**. These movement ideas may be arranged in any number of ways. Two popular forms in dance and music are **ABA** and **ABACA** (the latter is called "rondo" form). Inherent in both are the continuity of the recurring idea, **A**. Contrast is provided not only by the different natures of ideas **B** and **C** but by their placement in relation to idea **A**. For example, **A** could be skipping, **B** could be twirling in a circle, and **C** could be jumping with arms extended up. Using the idea of a simple rondo form, **ABACA**, the dance would then be:

A Everyone skips around in a circle

B Everyone twirls in place

A Everyone skips around in a circle

C Everyone jumps in place with arms extended up

A Everyone skips around in a circle

Suddenly, a dance is born, by organizing simple movement ideas into patterns. Ideas may be as simple or complex as you choose. The same is true for how you organize the ideas. Any sequence or combination is possible. For some children with disabilities, simply replicating one movement or sequencing two or three movements is a tremendous challenge. You can decide your own applications.

Form in dance, or in any of the arts, does not have to be complex or abstract. It is just a way of organizing ideas. If you choose to experiment with it in your movement activities, you will have begun to use the same basic process that any choreographer uses in creating a dance.

Why Not Just Movement?

Why not? There is nothing wrong in working with movement activities whether they become dances or not. You may feel that working with the idea of dance is too complex. You may be uncomfortable with movement activities and question their value and use with students who are barely capable of moving, much less remembering sequences of movement. However, working with basic movement activities is of great value, not only because of the physical benefits but because movement can be useful in developing intelligence.

The Elements of Dance

To understand dance and movement terminologies, it is easier to see them as they have been categorized rather than in an alphabetical listing. (Other terms are defined at the end of this section.) The four basic elements of dance movements are described in the following sections.

The Body

Parts of the Body

- **Outer**—head, shoulders, arms, hands, rib cage, hips, legs, feet, back
- **Inner**—organs (heart and lungs), muscles, bones, joints

Body Movements

Twisting

Bending

Stretching

Collapsing

Swaying

Swinging

Rising

Falling

Turning

Shaking

Steps

This refers to the moving of two feet in different rhythmic and spatial combinations. Movement through space is called "locomotion." Following are eight examples of steps:

1. *Walk*—A moderately paced transfer of weight from one foot to the other, as one moves through space.

2. *Run*—A relatively fast transfer of weight from one foot to the other, while moving through space.

3. *Leap*—A run with extended even steps off the ground.

4. *Hop*—An elevation using one foot (can move through space or be in one place).

5. *Jump*—An elevation using two feet (can move through space or be in one place).

6. *Skip*—A stepping hop that has an uneven beat or pulse.

7. *Gallop*—A leaping step that has an uneven beat or pulse.

8. *Slide*—An extended step, like the leap, but feet generally remain in contact with the ground.

Space

Space is the physical dimension through which the body moves. Shapes (designs or forms a body creates) can exist in space without moving from one place to another. Gestures can be bodily movements, also in one space area. However, when the body moves, each movement involves the following:

- *Direction*—A forward, backward, or sideways movement.

- *Size*—Big or small.

- *Focus*—An imaginary "destination" or point of concentration created by directing the eyes at a real or imaginary point in space.

- *Place*—The location in space where movement occurs.

- *Pathway*—The shape of imaginary lines on the ground. The two basic pathways in movement are based on straight and curved lines.

- *Levels*

    High

    Medium

    Low

Force

The same type of movement can be changed by varying the amount of energy, or the force, used to create that movement.

Elements of Force

- *Attack*—The way a movement is initiated. It can be sharp or smooth.

- *Weight*—It can be heavy or light.

- *Strength*—It can be weak or strong.

- *Flow*—It can be moving freely or more constricted.

Laban's Contribution to Movement Analysis

Rudolf von Laban, a dancer, choreographer, and teacher, revolutionized the dance world in the 1920s by inventing his own categories of movements and movement qualities. He also devised a way of symbolically notating movement so that choreographed dance pieces could be "read" and performed in much the same way as notated music is. It seems appropriate to list under the "force" category of dance movements Laban's list of what he called "stresses of movement":

1. *Pressing*—A strong, direct, and sustained energy.

2. *Wringing*—A strong, flexible, and sustained energy.

3. *Gliding*—A light, direct, and sustained energy.

4. *Floating*—A light, flexible, and sustained energy.

5. *Punching*—A strong, direct, and quick energy.

6. *Slashing*—A strong, flexible, and quick energy.

7. *Dabbing (or tapping)*—A light, direct, and quick energy.

8. *Flicking*—A light, flexible, and quick energy.

Time

Time is the duration that it takes for various movements to occur. In music, time considerations like beat (pulse), tempo, and rhythm refer to sound moving through time. Dance, which includes a physical body moving in and through space, has the same basic time elements:

- *Beat*—The basic pulse of the beat.
- *Tempo*—The rate of speed of the beat.
- *Duration*—Long and short periods of time in which movements occur.
- *Rhythm*—The organization of movement and stillness over longer and shorter periods of time. (Other dance vocabulary words can be found in the "Dance Glossary" at the end of this chapter.)

Using Music with Dance and Movement

Music can often be the inspiration for a dance. It can motivate children to move and inspire those who would otherwise have no inclination to move. At times, in your first movement explorations, silence can be less distracting to the creative exploratory process. However, added at the right time, music can be the magical element that makes your dance and movement activities come alive. It can give continuity to a sequence, set a mood, give rhythm to a movement, or just be a background for free dance. You may want to refer to the list of suggested music for dance activities on page 35.

Creating a Safe Space

1. To move in space, you must have sufficient space in which to move. If you do not have access to an auditorium, gym, or cafeteria, clear your own classroom by pushing chairs and desks to the side.

2. Students should be made aware that each individual has a personal space that should be respected. Physical contact should only occur if it is an integral part of an activity.

3. A level, wooden floor, free of splinters, is the ideal surface on which to move or dance. Concrete and asphalt could be dangerous. Even soft grass can be a slippery, uneven surface.

4. Comfortable footwear, preferably shoes with rubber soles, will help guard against slipping, falling, and foot injury.

5. In your movement exercises, warm-ups, and dances, keep a careful watch for students who appear fatigued or are straining to keep up. Also be aware of those who might become overly stimulated. Keep less demanding, alternative activities as options that can be quickly substituted if necessary.

Dance and Imagery

Imagery has always been an effective tool for teaching. In combination, imagery and movement can be powerful aids.

If you ask children to show you, using their bodies, a bird flying, the results are more like a drama exercise than a dance exercise. The children will be pantomiming a literal interpretation of a visual image. In contrast, the art form of dance is about movement, movement with different energy qualities through space and time. Requests to be "an ice cube melting" or "a seed growing" will usually produce dances that are really stories acted out with pantomime movements.

There are many teachers who might justifiably exclaim, "I would be ecstatic if that child could pretend to be a seed growing!" Certainly, imagery-oriented activities can be of considerable value in many situations. However, when working with the elements of dance, movement is first and imagery second.

Dance for Dance's Sake

Dance is movement of the body in relation to the space around it; it does not have to be about something. Frogs can jump and birds can fly, but arms can slice or drive through the air, bodies can bend, twist, and collapse, and hands can rise high into space. Dance does not have to be about something imagistic or narrative. Dance is about movement.

Using Imagery to Understand and Enhance Movement

Imagery can be used effectively to help understand a particular movement and improve the quality of that movement. This can happen when you use the word *like* in giving a direction that links movement and image. "Gallop *like* a wild horse" or "hop *like* a rabbit" helps to concretize the movement and intensifies the focus on the movement instead of the image.

If you say, "walk like a tiger," you should also say, "walk like an elephant," or "walk like a chicken" to keep the emphasis on the movement of *walking*, rather than on the image of an animal. Children must understand that what is being explored is walking. Tigers walk softly and smoothly, elephants walk heavily and slowly, chickens walk lightly and jerkily. All these different qualities of movement are the foundation upon which the art of dance is built.

"Stretch yourself thin and tall like a piece of grass," or "collapse like a popped balloon" are all directives that use imagery to explore movement. Ask the children, "How quickly can you collapse? How slowly? Can you collapse while you are moving through space?"

Movements Can Suggest Images

If a child is spinning, you might ask, "What moves (or spins) like this?" "A top or a carousel," he or she may answer. Using this way of wording the question, movement becomes the primary focus. Slashing movements may conjure up the image of hacking through the underbrush of a jungle. In all these examples, the image grows out of the movement, not the reverse.

General Warm-Ups for Any Movement Activity

Before any movement activity there should always be a warm-up. A general, but thorough, full body warm-up that stretches and moves all the body parts, muscles, and joints will help prevent injury, especially among children who move infrequently. With the heart pumping harder, circulation increased, joints and tendons loosened, and the body oxygenated from breathing more deeply, bodily awareness and neuromuscular coordination will be improved.

An ideal warm-up prepares the body and focuses the mind on the basic elements of the upcoming activity. Even though seriously involved students (that is, those with major issues or problems, whether physical, emotional, developmental, etc.) may not be able to perform activities that seem very strenuous, they too need some kind of gentle, physical warm-up to ease them into using their bodies in ways that lift them beyond the functional movements of their daily routine.

Considerations for Your Warm-Ups

1. All movements should be done slowly and without rushing.

2. It is best to model each warm-up movement for children.

3. Each movement should be repeated at least four times, if possible.

4. If using music, choose slower music, and play it softly. Teachers may want to count in a loud voice.

5. Modify any and all warm-ups and activity suggestions as needed. If standing doesn't work, sit. If sitting isn't possible, lie down.

6. Aides and other paraprofessional classroom facilitators can help children perform certain movements.

7. As usual, be flexible and find the value in what can be done rather than what can't.

How to Count for Warm-Ups

Counting the beats for your students' warm-ups is optional depending on your abilities and theirs.

Sample Warm-Up

Count "1, 2, 3, 4" in a steady beat while raising your left arm over your head. (Students will be "mirroring" you, so your *left* arm will be mirrored by the students' *right* arms.) Each movement should be done to a four count. You may practice with yourself in front of a mirror before trying it with the class.

Practice Step 1

Have students raise their right arms over their heads as you count "1, 2, 3, 4" and raise your left arm. By the count of four, their arms should be straight up. Have them lower their right arms back to their sides as you count "1, 2, 3, 4." By the count of four, their arms should be back at their sides. If they can do this easily, go on to the next step.

7

Practice Step 2

Do the same as Step 1 in four complete cycles. This time substitute the word *up* for count one as you go upwards and *down* for count one as you go downwards. Start with your right arm at your side. Raise your right arm as you count "up, 2 ,3, 4." Lower your right arm as you count "down, 2, 3, 4." This counts as one cycle. Try each cycle four times:

Up 2 3 4

Down 2 3 4 (one cycle)

Up 2 3 4

Down 2 3 4 (two cycles)

etc.

Practice Step 3

If you are feeling comfortable you can add words. No matter what you say, *up* should be on "1" and *down* should be on "1"; for example:

"Now up 2, 3, 4"

"And down 2, 3, 4"

"And up 2, 3, 4"

"Now down 2, 3, 4"

When working with other movements and body parts, simply substitute the appropriate word for count "1," "side, 2, 3, 4," or "to the side, 2, 3, 4." You can make up your own formula to communicate with your students.

Stretching the Muscles and Tendons

Do whichever movements are possible with your students. Count, or be flexible with the time it takes them to complete one movement. Just remember to move slowly and carefully and try to repeat each movement four times.

Movements to Stretch Muscles

1. Stretch the right arm up and over the head as described above. Lower it down to the side. Do the same with the left arm. Try it with both arms together.

2. Bend over, stretch down, and touch the toes with both hands. Stand back up.

3. Stretch both arms straight out to the sides. With outstretched arms, twist to the right and then to the left. Keep the feet stationary.

4. Sit on the floor with legs stretched wide. Touch the right ankle with both hands. Touch the left ankle with both hands. Extend the legs straight in front. Try to touch both ankles with both hands (try to keep the legs straight without bending the knees).

5. With hands on hips, bend sideways to the right and back to center. Bend sideways to the left and back to center.

6. Stand or sit with the arms at the sides, looking straight ahead. Stretch the neck by tilting the head to the right and then to the left.

7. Now turn the head to the right and back to the front. Turn to the left and again to the front.

8. Tilt the head back to stretch the front of the neck and tilt the head down to stretch the back of the neck.

Movements to Loosen Joints and Tendons

Remember to do each movement slowly. Try to repeat each movement four times, if possible, before going on. Many of these movements can be done from a sitting position.

1. Rotate the head slowly to the right. Rotate the head slowly to the left.
2. "Shake out" the head by nodding and rolling loosely in different directions.
3. Shrug the shoulders up and then down.
4. Rotate the shoulders back and then forward.
5. Hold the right arm straight but loose and rotate it forward from the shoulder joint. Do the same with the left arm.
6. Wiggle the fingers of both hands with the arms at the sides.
7. Rotate the wrists of both hands.
8. "Shake out" the hands (a fast, loose shaking motion).
9. With the arms hanging loose, "shake out" the fingers, hands, and arms.
10. Wiggle the toes of both feet.
11. Rotate the right ankle. Rotate the left ankle.
12. Lift leg and bend the right knee. Lift and bend the left knee.
13. Rotate the hips.
14. "Shake out" the entire body, including the head.

You can ask children with severe disabilities to move their eyes, to blink, to open and close their mouths, wiggle their fingers, or move any other part of their bodies. With varied ranges of ability, what is a warm-up, a movement activity, or a dance depends on the capabilities of individual students.

Movement Activities That Also Warm Up

There are many fun and gamelike movement activities. They ease the students into moving their bodies while not demanding a great deal of any one student. These activities are rich with the seeds of ideas for more complex movements and dances.

The Movement Name Game

This is a very rich warm-up. What once began as a theater game has been adapted as a warm-up or activity in almost every art form. As much as it has been used, it will probably be new to your students. It will help your students speak their names and possibly the names of others. It will encourage them to express something about themselves with their bodies. As usual, make modifications based on what will work for your students.

Activity Process

Estimated Time: One session or part of one session.

Suggested Music: Music is not necessary and may be distracting.

Level

Useful for students who can speak their names and make at least one movement with their bodies.

Benefits

- Understanding self in relation to movement
- Linguistic skill by speaking their names
- Memory for sequences of movements
- Fine and/or gross motor coordination

Directions

1. Have students stand in a circle.

2. Go around the circle and have each person say his or her name. After each name is said, have the class repeat it in unison, if possible.

3. After going around once, have students take a moment to think about themselves: how they are feeling, who they are, or something they know about themselves.

4. Tell them you are going around the circle as before and each person is to say his or her name. This time, however, each person should add one movement that expresses something about himself or herself. If students can say their names and move at the same time, they should. If they cannot, they should move first and then speak their names.

5. As each person says his or her name and makes a movement, have the class repeat it like an echo.

6. The next time around the circle, use only the movements.

Variations

1. Ask students if they remember anyone else's name and movement. Have them demonstrate.

2. Have a student "do" his or her name and movement first, then do someone else's name and movement. That person then does his or her own and someone else's.

3. Using movement only, go around the circle as quickly as possible, each person performing his or her movement as soon as the previous person is finished. Reverse, and do this quickly in the other direction.

4. Choose a leader or "conductor" to stand in the center of the circle. You might want to help the conductor (and other students, who will be the next conductors) decide on some physical gestures that will nonverbally stop or start each student.

The conductor can point to anyone in the circle to "do" his or her movement one time. Following are some of the choices the conductor might make:

1. Point to different people at random to do their movements once.

2. Point quickly around the circle at one person at a time, then reverse direction.

3. Have one person repeat a movement over and over.

4. Have one person repeat a movement over and over while the group does that movement just once.

5. Start with one person repeating a movement over and over and gradually add others one at a time until everyone is doing his or her own movement repeatedly. Reverse the process to stop moving, one at a time, until only one person is left moving.

6. Explore various combinations of:

   Solo—one person moving

   Duet—two people moving

   Trio—three people moving

   Quartet—four people moving (etc.)

Movement Machine

This exercise explores individual repeated movements, levels in space, and sculptural shapes created by combining moving bodies in a stationary space.

Activity Process

Estimated Time: 10–20 minutes

Suggested Music: If music is used, it is better to use it while the machine itself is being created for the second time. In the beginning, having no music allows students to make movement choices and find their own sense of rhythm and beat in their movements. Creating the movement machine without the music the first time it is done keeps the focus on the shape of many bodies moving together.

Level

Students need not be able to speak but should be able to understand directions. They should be able to make at least one single movement and have the physical stamina to repeat it over and over for a short period of time. Students should also be able to move (with assistance if necessary) from the perimeter of the circle to the center.

Benefits

- Fine and/or gross motor coordination
- Cognitive ability in following directions
- Creativity in making movement choices based on spatial perception
- Perception of sculptural body shapes moving in space

Directions

1. Have students stand or sit in a circle facing the center.

2. Go around the circle and have each student make just one movement that he or she can repeat with ease.

3. After everyone has shown his or her movement, have one volunteer go to the center of the circle. Adult aides may have to help.

4. The student in the center performs his or her movement repeatedly without stopping.

5. Students chosen by you move, one at a time, to the center of the circle and add their movements to the growing movement machine. *It is not necessary to touch anyone in the machine,* but the new person should feel and look as though he or she is attaching

himself or herself to it. To achieve this, encourage the students to move close to one another in the center.

6. Each person who moves to the center performs his or her movement repeatedly.

7. Encourage students to think of levels in space by deciding whether they want to perform their movements low in space and be a lower part of the machine or move higher in space to be a higher part of the machine.

Variations

1. Construct a movement machine once more, but this time, use music as soon as the circle is formed. Students will probably naturally adapt the speed and rhythms of their movement to the music.

2. Take a photograph or make a videotape of your movement machine so students may reflect back on the experience and perceive what they created.

3. If you use the movement machine as a warm-up, on different days it could have different themes. You may work with such ideas as

   Low, medium, and high levels in space

   Movements that are fast or slow

   Movements that are big or small

   Movements made while holding the body stiff and straight

   Movements made while holding the body loose and curved

   Movements made with only one specific body part

4. Divide the class into two or three groups. Have each group take turns making a movement machine for the other group of students to observe. As a game challenge, you may give each group a secret movement theme such as "high levels in space" and have the rest of the class guess the theme of the movement machine.

Traveling Through Space: Modes of Locomotion

Although this activity may seem simplistic at first, students enjoy it. It allows them to experience a variety of ways to move through space.

Activity Process

Estimated Time: Part of a session if a warm-up; an entire session if used to explore locomotion.

Suggested Music: Use music that fits the tempo (speed) and the character of locomotion being used (see "Music for Dance Activities" at the end of this chapter).

Level

Students who can perform different modes of locomotion and students who use wheelchairs. Small groups of semi-ambulatory children can be assisted through space by adult helpers.

Benefits

- Gross motor coordination
- Perception of movement in relation to space
- Understanding of modes of locomotion

Eight Modes of Locomotion

Decide which of the following to use with your students. Because this activity needs space through which to travel, gym floors might be the best location.

- Walking

- Jumping

- Running

- Skipping

- Leaping

- Galloping

- Hopping

- Sliding

Directions

1. At one end of the gym, have students form a straight line facing the far end of the gym.

2. At your signal, everyone should walk (gallop, skip, etc.) together, staying in a line, to the other end of the gym. Then they should turn around and face the other end. They should all be using the same mode of locomotion.

3. At your signal, have students go back, perhaps using a different mode of locomotion, and then turn around again.

4. You may do this many times, using as many different modes of locomotion as possible.

Children who use wheelchairs can be moved through space by adults in the following ways:

1. Fast or slow

2. Forward or backward

3. In gentle stops and starts

Ambulatory students may be helped through space by adults. This works best one at a time, using short distances to travel.

Variations

The idea of imagery, and bodily response to the images, will facilitate the exploration of traveling through space. Try to create your own metaphors based on your students' physical capabilities. If students are walking, give them different directives, such as

- Walk like a mouse;

- Walk like an elephant;

- Walk like a cat; or

- Walk like a man on stilts.

By going through each mode of locomotion this way, students will see and experience not only the differences between various ways of traveling through space but also different ways to execute a single mode of locomotion.

Exploring Pathways

This is a simple warm-up activity. It does not substitute for a full body general warm-up. It can be an entire session, depending on how you use these ideas.

Pathways are straight or curved. We follow them on the ground. When these pathways enclose a space on the ground, a geometric shape is created. Straight pathways can create the enclosed shapes of triangles, squares, or rectangles. Curved pathways create ovals, circles, spirals, or figure-eights. An open gym floor is best for this activity and music is optional. Make students aware that each person has his or her own personal space that should be respected. Students will be moving freely on pathways they create. Emphasize that they should try to steer clear of other students.

Activity Process

Estimated Time: One session or more.

Suggested Music: Optional—only use after directions are clear. See "Music for Dance Activities" at the end of this chapter. Also, a drum beat could played by a teacher or an aide.

Level

Students need to be ambulatory enough to walk and should see well enough to understand the idea of straight and curving lines and various geometric shapes. (See adaptations in "Activities for Severely and Multiply Disabled Children," page 21.)

Benefits

- Sense of body in relation to other bodies
- Perception of geometric and organic shapes

Directions

1. Have each student find his or her own space anywhere on the floor.

2. Instruct students to walk on a straight pathway. If they need to turn, the turn must be angular. Model both movements or just the turn. Show them a pathway that zigzags.

3. Instruct students to walk on curving pathways. Demonstrate how curves turn smoothly and how spirals may be created.

4. Divide the class into two groups. Have one group follow a straight or curved pathway while the other group watches. (Use masking tape to make a straight line and a curved line on the gym floor.)

Variations

1. If students are able, have them run, skip, jump, etc., on straight or curved pathways.

2. Have one group of students move on straight pathways and another group on curved pathways simultaneously.

3. Have students follow each other in a line as a leader takes them on a straight or curved pathway.

Working with Shapes

You may want to review shapes with forms drawn on paper first before asking students to identify these shapes on a floor.

1. Using masking tape, create a circle, a figure-eight, a square, a triangle, and a rectangle on the gym floor.

2. Ask students to identify as many of the shapes as they can.

3. Ask them which shapes use straight lines and which use curved lines.

4. You may want to start with the circle shape. Following are some possibilities for using a circle:

    Walk around on the taped shape of the circle.

    Run, or use other modes of locomotion on the taped shape of the circle.

    Jump in and out of the circle.

    Move only inside the circle space.

    Move freely outside the circle space.

    Jump over it.

    Add your own creative ways of moving within the circle.

5. Do Step 4 within all of the possible geometric shapes. You can add spirals or zigzags or create your own free forms.

Free Dance

Free dance, or improvisatory dance, is the spontaneous choreography and performance of movement ideas. Although this sounds like a sophisticated process (and actually is), it is what children do all the time when they dance to music. Free dance, though not a planned dance, can be used as an idea in a planned dance form. For example, in an **ABA** dance form, idea **A** could be a planned movement or movements, and idea **B** could be free dance, with idea **A,** planned, returning again. There are several ways to make free dance more than just random movement. Your own creativity will help you come up with even more ideas.

Activity Process

Estimated Time: Can be one session, or part of one session.

Suggested Music: See directions.

Level

If you can substitute the word "movement" for "dance," any child could move freely to music however he or she is able, or with assistance.

Benefits

- Self-expression
- Physical and emotional release of energy
- Creative use of bodily kinesthetic intelligence

Directions

1. Choose a particular piece of music, or music from a particular culture or genre (pop, rock, jazz, classical, folk, etc.).

2. You can beat a drum with a steady pulse or rhythm and students can move to that. If you have classroom instruments, you can have some students play beats or rhythms as background for classmates' free dance.

3. Take one specific type of movement, like sliding. Explore it in different ways with different parts of the body. Have students free dance using only sliding movements. Depending on your students' abilities, you can use more than one type of movement in your free dance activity.

4. Take one specific type of locomotion and explore it in a warm-up. Free dance to music that uses one type of locomotion movement incorporated into the dance, such as jumping or skipping.

5. Explore all levels in space from high to low.

6. Free dance with partners. Free dance in groups of three or four. Perform for one another.

Note: Free dance does not mean "a free for all," although at times that too can serve a purpose of release after a hard day of more structured movement activity. Provide some guidelines, suggestions, and parameters in free dance so that there is focus and a chance for creative discovery. Use your own ideas so that free dance can best benefit your students.

Imagery as a Source of Movement and Dance

What Am I Passing?

This activity stimulates imagination, movement, and interaction with others. In it, movements are created by passing an imaginary object around a circle. The movement will then be detached from the image idea that inspired it and explored as pure movement. If your students cannot visualize an imaginary object, use real objects at first to pass around the circle.

Activity Process

Estimated Time: One session for passing objects, more sessions if movements are progressed to dances.

Suggested Music: None for the passing activity. Focus should be on visualization and movement.

In the first part of this activity, the passing of the object (or idea object) can serve as a mini warm-up.

Level

Children should be able to use their hands and arms to pass an imaginary or real object. They should also have some ability to visualize, or imagine, the physical characteristics of the object (a light feather, a heavy stone).

For children who cannot visualize an imaginary object but have the physical ability to pass a real object, you might bring things to class (small enough to be handled easily) with different weights, sizes, textures, shapes, smells, and temperatures. Children should pass the real object first to find their movement. The object should then be removed so that the second time around the circle, students are making only the movement without the real object. The focus should then turn to the movement itself.

Using the imaginary object activity will strengthen imagination and visualization abilities of students with this potential. Many children will need to start with an actual physical object. Assess your children's abilities and adapt these options accordingly.

Benefits

- Fine and gross motor coordination
- Ability to visualize an imaginary object
- Ability to respond kinesthetically to an imaginary (or real) object
- Perception of different ways to make movements in space as influenced by real or imaginary physical considerations
- Perception of movement for movement's sake detached from an image idea
- Ability to remember and perform short sequences of movements
- Perception of patterns in the way movement ideas are organized
- Interpersonal relating through physical movement

Object Ideas

In these activities, use as many of the ideas below as you choose. The different qualities of the objects should evoke different movement responses.

For children who *can* visualize imaginary objects, you might "pass around"

A rotten egg

A feather

A baby chick

An ice cube

A hot potato

A heavy stone

A smelly sock

Sand

A writhing snake

A flower

Real objects for children who *cannot* visualize imaginary objects include

A ball

A feather or a piece of thread

Sand (or gravel or marbles)

Something light and large, square or rectangular, like a cardboard box

A heavy stone

A sock

A living animal (remind children to be careful when handling a living creature)

A silk scarf

A piece of ice

A flower

Preparing for the Activity

Although the activity could be a warm-up itself, stretching and moving body parts, as described in the general warm-up section, are always a good idea.

You might feel more comfortable leading this activity if you visualize and practice some of the movements ahead of time. By looking at your own movements in passing a real or imaginary feather, you may decide how to model this for your students.

Some of Laban's movement classifications may evolve from the original passing movements:

- Pressing
- Punching
- Wringing
- Slashing
- Gliding
- Dabbing
- Floating
- Flicking

The movement used for passing a feather could be exaggerated and evolve to a floating movement. Then the idea of floating can be explored. Passing a writhing snake could be altered slightly to be a wringing movement.

Directions

1. Have students stand (or sit) in a circle close enough together to be able to reach over to the person next to them.

2. From your list of imaginary or real objects, choose one "object" to pass around the circle.

3. Begin by having one student pass the object around the circle to the student next to him or her. If an imaginary object is used, you may have to model a movement to get things started. Help infuse the process with a sense of reality by allowing yourself to respond physically and emotionally to the object being passed. If a real object is used, go around a second time, making the movements without the object. Remind students to use the same or similar movements as they did when passing the real object.

4. Have students pass an object once more, this time focusing solely on the movement. The original movement can be changed slightly or exaggerated. The gentle flowing gesture of passing a flower could be expanded into a larger gesture that uses the entire arm. Retain some of the original energy, emotion, and quality of movement that occurred the first time around.

5. Repeat the same process with another contrasting object, real or imaginary. If the first object was a feather, the next might be a hot potato or a stone. Note how movements not only differ from object to object but also from student to student.

6. Go around the circle again, focusing only on movement.

7. Now take one of the movements, such as passing the "writhing snake." How would you describe the movement: twisty, slow, and smooth? Is it a large and expansive or more contained movement?

Ball-Passing Variations

An object may be passed in different ways. A ball, for example, has many possibilities. Try using an imaginary ball if possible; if not, carefully pass a real ball once around the circle. Experiment with different ways of transferring the ball to another person. (See list below.)

Now, put the ball aside. The next time around the circle, students can pretend they have the ball and can try getting it to another person in the circle by

- rolling,
- tossing, or
- bouncing.

Ask the students to suggest other ways of passing the ball.

For this exercise it may be interesting to look at or call out the name of someone anywhere in the circle and pass the ball to him or her. Have everyone first explore only one way of passing the ball. For example, students can first explore the movement of rolling it. This involves a forward arm movement and a positioning of the body lower in space. The movement of throwing the imaginary ball very fast could be called a slashing or driving movement. Students enjoy this movement because they can release the energy of throwing an imaginary ball very fast without breaking anything.

Activity Progression: Creating Simple Dances

Now that you have a small but well-explored group of movement ideas, you may begin to use some of these ideas to create a simple dance. (See "What Makes a Dance?" on page 2.)

One of the simplest forms in dance or music is one that takes two ideas, **A** and **B**, and organizes them into the plan of **ABA**:

- Main idea.
- New idea contrasting with **A**.
- Main idea returns.

The **ABA** form provides contrast and unity and is a planned form rather than a free or improvised form.

To keep the dance simple you can work with one movement idea, such as floating. Before committing to movement ideas for your **ABA** form, first explore floating with your students:

1. Have everyone try floating movements with different parts of their bodies: fingers, hands, arms, head, both arms, legs, torso, etc.

2. Remember that a dance has to have three basic components:

   Movement,

   Movement idea(s), and

   A plan.

3. You can begin by creating two different movement ideas that both use the idea of floating. For example:

   Idea A: Everyone floats around the circle with both arms extended to the sides.

   Idea B: Everyone stops, faces center, floats to the center of the circle and back.

4. The simple **ABA** dance would then be:

   Idea A: Everyone floats around the circle with both arms extended to the sides.

   Idea B: At a signal, everyone stops, faces center, and floats to the center of the circle and back.

Idea A: Everyone floats around the circle with both arms extended to the sides.

5. *Remember:*

Always rehearse each movement idea first before transforming it into a dance.

When changing from a repetitive movement, like floating around a circle, you will need some kind of signal (aural or visual) to change to the next idea, **B**. In this dance, the movement in **B** has a definite end to it, so a signal is optional before returning to the movement of **A**.

Children can help come up with ideas for the sections and will be pleased when they can perform and see others perform their ideas.

ABA form may also use a different form of movement, other than that of floating in **A**, for the **B** section.

Extending Your Dance

Form in dance is created by the way movement ideas are organized. The following activities are two simple ways of taking ideas you have already worked with and creating a longer, more extended dance. The complexity of your dance ideas and forms will be determined by your understanding and creativity and by students' abilities. Feel free to use any movement ideas in your own dance forms.

Make a Longer ABA Dance

1. Make your **A** section longer by taking your previous **ABA** dance (above) and making that entire sequence of three ideas into a longer idea **A**.

2. **B** would be a totally new idea, preferably contrasting, since your old **B** is now part of a bigger **A** section. Section **B** could be free dance with spinning movements.

3. All dances need an ending, so it is common to add to your repeated **A** a short movement idea that brings your dance to a satisfying close. In this case, it could be as simple as freezing in place at a signal with both arms stretched up over the head. (In music, this is called a *coda*, an extended "tailpiece" to your dance.)

Create a "Rondo" Form Dance

By adding a third idea, **C**, and using the "rondo" form sequence of ideas, **ABACA**, the dance becomes more extended. If idea **C** is that one student at a time or as many as three or more students free dance in the center of the circle using floating or slashing movements, your new dance would be as follows:

A—Everyone floats around the circle with arms extended to the sides.

At a signal, everyone stops, faces center, floats to the center and back.

At a signal, everyone floats around the circle with both arms extended to the sides.

B—At a signal, everyone free dances in place using spinning movements.

A—At a signal, repeat all of **A**.

C—At a signal, one person at a time free dances in the center of the circle, using floating or spinning movements, while everyone claps in time.

A—At a signal, repeat **A**.

Ending (*at signal*)—Everyone freezes in place with arms stretched up over their heads.

Adaptations for Severely Disabled Children

Remember that form in dance is nothing more than a sequence and arrangement of movement ideas. For children with little movement ability, these activities can be gamelike and motivational for developing bodily kinesthetic awareness and coordination, as well as learning simple sequences of movements. You can choose movements that address those areas where your students need help.

Example:
Idea A—Wiggle fingers.
Idea B—Shake head.

ABA form would then be: **Idea A**—Wiggle fingers.
                                Idea B—Shake head.
                                Idea A—Wiggle fingers

Adding **Idea C** as flapping arms,   **Idea A**—Wiggle fingers.
a "rondo form" would then be: **Idea B**—Shake head.
                                       Idea A—Wiggle fingers.
                                       Idea C—Flap arms.
                                       Idea A—Wiggle fingers

Music in the background can add fun and be a rewarding addition to a correctly learned sequence of movement.

Using Music

When you are creating a dance, it is sometimes best to first work out the understanding and coordination of an actual movement without music. Once you have the movement idea, you can rehearse it with music. Then you can work on another movement idea without music. The beat and rhythm inspire the movements that you have already decided to use. As you recall, in this activity, imagery was the original source of movement ideas, although you may come up with your own way of finding movement ideas. In other activities, such as movement to African music, movement ideas are strongly related to the music.

Please refer to the music list for ideas. Floating movements may work well with slower music. Slashing movements might work better with faster music.

Adding music after working out movements will often amaze and surprise students. Movement sequences are suddenly validated by the music and become a real dance.

Activities for Severely and Multiply Disabled Children

Body sensations of moving and feeling movement reaffirm a child's sense of being alive. The colors of props, the sounds of the music, and the experience of moving or of being moved can encourage more independence and autonomy to move in everyday life.

Level

Severe involvement, multiple disabilities. *These activities require adequate adult assistance, preferably one-on-one.*

Benefits

• Motor coordination

- Motivation to move and be involved in the process of movement
- Perception of the relationship between hearing music and feeling and initiating movement
- Perception of seeing the visual results of movement
- Perception of pathways in space, directions, and levels in space
- Motivation and reinforcement of language that refers to movement and space

Silk Scarf, Balloon, or Feather Dance

Activity Process

Estimated Time: One session.

Suggested Music: Graceful, flowing music seems to work best with this activity. (See "Music for Dance Activities," page 35.) Folk music on harp or dulcimer, or new age or Native American flute music, provides a light, ongoing, floating feeling that will reflect the visual props being used and the resulting movements.

Level

This activity is for children with severe or multiple disabilities who may have very little movement ability other than eye movement or minimal hand or finger coordination.

Materials

Brightly colored, small scarves (or pieces of material cut into scarf-sized squares) or brightly colored balloons attached by string to the end of a chopstick, ice cream stick, etc. Large colorful feathers, such as ostrich or peacock feathers, may also be used. (**Note:** If you use balloons, attach them to the stick with three to six inches of thread or string to help create more fluid movements.)

Directions

1. Have students sit or lie comfortably. Adult helpers should position themselves comfortably behind or to the side of the students. Staying out of the front line of vision will allow students to focus on the movement of the object in front of them.

2. With one-on-one adult assistance, place a stick with its brightly colored attachment into each child's hand. If he or she can't hold it alone, help the student hand over hand.

3. Play the music of your choice. Work alongside the child, helping him or her to hold and move the prop to the music, using faster or slower, bigger or smaller, smoother or jerkier movements.

4. Try moving the prop in different directions: side to side, up and down, and back and forth. If the child can understand, encourage him or her to follow the movement of the colored prop with his or her eyes.

5. As the child begins to pay attention to the movement of the prop and realize how it is being moved, ease him or her into holding and moving the prop alone. If the child cannot, you may continue to provide assistance.

6. If some children are capable of holding the prop, you might give them another.

7. If some children are ambulatory, let them walk and move their props to the music. This activity can provide a sense of connection among visual, physical, and aural sensations.

Wheelchair Dances: Direction, Pathways, and Shapes

Activity Process

Estimated Time: One session

Suggested Music: Music can be slow to moderate in speed. (See "Music for Dance Activities" on page 35.) Tchaikovsky's *Waltz Serenade* and other waltzes, Pachelbel's *Canon*, marches, or other music with regular rhythms and strong melodies will work well.

Level

With help, children using wheelchairs can experience directions, pathways, and shapes in much the same way a dancer might.

Special Requirements

This activity will require a large, open space like a gymnasium floor, as well as one adult per child using a wheelchair. The aides should be willing to move the children in wheelchairs during the full length of the activity.

Following is a list of movement options that adult aides may use as a guide for moving the wheelchairs while the music is playing. It can simplify the attending adults' task if everyone experiences the same movement at the same time. Music may be changed at any time to reflect changes in the movement activities.

- Speeds: slow to moderately fast.
- Directions: forward, backward, diagonal.
- Pathways: straight lines, zigzags, angled turns, spirals, curved and wavy lines.
- Shapes: squares, rectangles, triangles, circles, figure-eights.

Directions

1. Play the music of your choice.

2. Line up the wheelchairs next to one another at one end of the gym.

3. With music, move the wheelchairs in a line to the other end of the gym. Without reversing the position of the chairs, walk backwards to the original position. If possible, reinforce the concepts of *forward* and *backward*.

4. With the chairs again next to one another, have one chair at each end of the line move in a straight diagonal line to the opposite corner. The two chairs will pass one another in the middle. When these two chairs are in position forming the two ends of a new line, the next two chairs at either end of the original line will follow the same diagonal path. Continue this process until the new line is formed.

5. Using all the open space on the floor, explore moving in all directions using pathways of straight lines. Marches or other music with a regular rhythm are good for this. Then try moving in zigzags and in shorter straight lines with 90 degree turns.

6. Use bright yellow or other tape to create geometric shapes on the floor: squares, rectangles, and triangles. Explore the shapes one at a time, following the outline or going in or out of the shape. Encourage students to note each shape and if possible say its name.

7. Using all the open space on the floor, explore moving in curved lines. Waltzes or other flowing music are good for this. Trace a wave on the floor. Follow paths of large curves, small curves, and spirals. (The lines on the floor add visual stimulus and help visual and spacial intelligence.)

8. Using tape, make the outlines of larger and smaller circles and figure-eights on the floor. Again, explore one shape at a time, following the outline of the shape and going in and out of it. Students should be visually aware of the shape they are relating to with movement and should say the name of the shape if possible.

Note: When the wheelchairs are moved along the outline, or in and out of taped shapes on the floor, students may be given a ball or a square block to hold. They may hold whatever three-dimensional object reflects the shape. Small cut-out shapes in bright colors, or colored shapes outlined on large white index cards, may be given to students as each shape is explored. You may use the written word also if applicable to your goals and your students' abilities.

Free Dance

Play any music of your choice, from African, Latin, or jazz to the first movement of a Beethoven symphony. Adult aides can move chairs in a free response to the music, using all the available floor space. Encourage students to be involved in movement choices in whatever way they are able. Using words like *fast, slow, forward,* and *backwards,* or even holding up cards of straight lines, curved lines, or different shapes may encourage a student to participate in movement choices.

Special Explorations: Stop-Go, High-Low, Fast-Slow, Over-Under

Use of the classroom is acceptable for this activity as long as the group is small and there is room to move in lines and pathways around desks and chairs. Maneuvering between objects like furniture can be part of the fun.

Activity Process

Estimated Time: One or more sessions

Suggested Music: You may use recorded music if you like. However, you can also beat a drum, tap rhythm sticks, or clap a steady beat while repeatedly chanting one word. Playing guitar and strumming a simple chord while walking would also work well.

Level

This activity is best for lower functioning or students with multiple disabilities who are ambulatory or semi-ambulatory with assistance. Some students may need attendant adults to help balance them as they attempt to move.

Directions: Stop and Go

1. Begin your music, clapping or beating a drum in a regular rhythm while chanting "walk, walk, walk, walk" over and over. Lead the line while you beat and chant and have the children follow you.

2. When you feel like it, shout "STOP!" and freeze. Students should also freeze. After a moment say "Go!" and everyone will begin following.

3. After students understand the activity, you may choose one student to call "Stop" and "Go." The motivation for saying "Stop" and "Go" becomes very powerful because by saying it the student is controlling the class. Even students who understand "Stop"

and "Go" but cannot speak it intelligibly will call out a sound that obviously means "Stop" at the appropriate time.

Variations

High and Low

1. Follow the previous procedure but substitute "high" and "low" instead of "stop" and "go." Walking is still the safest mode of locomotion for this variation.

2. As you clap or beat the drum, chant "high, high, high, high" over and over. Students should walk as tall as possible with arms extended upward. When you are ready, change to "low, low, low, low" and lead the class, moving in a lower, crouching position.

3. Choose a student leader to make the calls of "high" and "low."

Fast and Slow

1. This will also be done to a clap or drumbeat. Chant "fast, fast" or "slow, slow," making your beat reflect the speed at which you would like everyone to move. If you are beating, chanting, and moving fast (not too fast), when you say "slow," immediately and exaggeratedly slow down.

2. Again, pick student leaders or encourage students to call out the directives of "fast" and "slow" to control the movement of the class.

Over and Under

1. Have two students or aides hold a piece of rope or brightly colored ribbon two to four inches off the ground. Have the students line up one behind the other. Using your clap or beat or chant of "over, over, over, over," lead your students in stepping, one at a time, over the rope or ribbon.

2. Then change the chant to "under, under." The rope holders should then raise the rope to a position slightly lower than the children's heads so that they will have to lower their bodies to pass under the rope.

Work with objects in your environment to create other activities with movements and sounds that explore other spatial concepts such as *in and out* and *around and through*. For example, if you have a large cardboard box, students may stand in line, and while you beat or clap and chant "in, in, in, in," one student might crawl into the box. When you or another student says "out!" the student would come out.

Doing these simple activities to the rhythms of claps, drumbeats, chants, or other music makes the activities stimulating, motivating, and gamelike.

Exploring Movement with African Music

Children with special needs can move to African music in activities that, although simple and adaptable, are inspired by African values and sensibilities. If you are aware, even in the most basic way, of African practices and perspectives, working with your students will have an integrity stemming from your own understanding of and respect for the culture.

Activity Process

Estimated Time: One or more of these activities may be done in a single session. The order can be kept and divided into shorter sequential segments. Adapt as you see fit.

Suggested Music: See "African Dance Music" on page 37.

Level

With modifications, all levels of students can experience the invigorating and uplifting power of African music. This music by its nature is strongly linked to physicality; and the human body can be stimulated to respond with movement to the beats and rhythms of the drums.

For severely disabled students, head movements, finger movements, eye movements, twitching of the shoulders, or vocal emissions may occur when this music is played. Blind students may move in free improvisation alone or with a partner. Deaf students may dance barefoot on a floor that might carry the vibration of the speakers, or dance with a hearing partner. Beating a real drum very near them in time to the music and letting children touch it can give them a basic sense of the beat. Some call and response ideas can be adapted to a simpler motion that someone moving a wheelchair could make. Likewise, wheelchair partner dances, using the idea of dialogue, can be fun. Children using wheelchairs also enjoy seeing others move to the music. Even though they may not be initiating the movement themselves, there is a satisfaction in being able to feel their bodies moving through space.

Benefits

- Motivation to move
- Ability to perform short sequences of movements
- Ability to assume a leadership role
- Fine and gross motor coordination
- Bodily kinesthetic response to rhythm
- Ability to create as well as replicate body movements
- Perception of the link between physical movement and rhythm in music
- Ability to interact and integrate on a physical level, with an individual or group

A Note About African Music

To the African way of thinking, dancing is visible proof that the dancer understands, or "hears," the music with the body. African dance also uses many parts of the body to reflect the different rhythms (called polyrhythms) occurring simultaneously in the music. A tribal chief in the Cameroons expressed the thought that only when a dancer is really listening to the drums can he truly begin to dance. Only then will his body become an echo of what the drum is playing.

Although Western dance sometimes uses emotion or imagery for movement ideas, in African dance, it is largely the rhythm of the drums that is the inspiration for physical expression. Symbolically, the drums represent the spirit voices of the ancestors who keep a vigil over the life of the village. To dance and drum in the "right" way is inspired by the esteem and gratitude for the ancestral spirits who help perpetuate the moral spirit of life and tradition in the community.

African Dance Practices That Parallel Classroom Movement Activities

If your class has been practicing movement activities, you may want to point out some of these parallels in a very simple way. If the students cannot understand, at least you will have the experience of seeing these movement activities with African music from a broader cultural perspective.

1. African dance has a strong improvisatory element that is based on the dancers' responses to the drums' rhythms. In "free dancing" or "free expression" as separate activities or in the context of a larger activity, the students' physical responses to the drums' rhythms will also be improvisatory.

2. In African dance, some dancers add their own movements in rhythms that are not being played on the drums. Instead of viewing this as a "mistake," Africans consider this a creative contribution to the whole experience. In your students' free dance to the drumming music, they may add their own movements that at times will not seem to relate to the music. Consider this their creative contribution. The Africans see it as filling in open spaces in the music, not a lack of coordination or ability. During times of free dancing, tell your students that they are to listen intently to the rhythms of the drums and dance to that. But make sure they are told also that all their creative "contributions" are welcome and appreciated by everyone in the group, especially you.

3. Because there is so much going on rhythmically in African dance music, dancers will often make sure that some part of their body keeps a steady beat or a short rhythm pattern of movements going so that there is a reference point.

4. With so many simultaneous polyrhythms, African dancers use different body parts to express the many different rhythms they hear. Some of your warm-ups will include moving isolated body parts to the rhythms of the music.

5. Circle dances, as in African dance, will use improvisation as well as the idea of "call and response." In a circle dance involving a large group of people, a leader makes a "call" (a movement and a chant) alone, and the group makes a "response" by either exactly repeating the leader's call or answering differently. In any case, the group response is in unison, that is, doing exactly the same movement, or movement plus sound, at the exact same time. The leader will then do another call and the group will respond. Calls and leaders can change in classroom activities.

6. Partner dance activities will also reflect various African dance practices. In African music, drums often carry on a "dialogue," playing rhythms back and forth. The relationship between the dancers and the drum rhythms is also considered a kind of dialogue. Partner dances can reflect a dialogue or "movement conversation" between the two dancing partners.

7. "Someone is always watching you" is an old African folk saying. Because African dance is communal, African rituals, dances, and festivities are not complete unless there are appreciative spectators. Partner dances and circle dances are both conducive to being seen by the participants themselves. Make sure that when one part of the class views the other part, roles change from that of creator and performer to that of spectator.

Warm-Up to African Music

Begin with the standard warm-up of body stretching and moving. You may need to make adaptations to the suggested formation for your students in the African music warm-up. If lying on the floor is not a good idea for your class, find standing or sitting positions where students are not facing one another.

1. Have students stand in a circle facing outward, away from the center. Ideally, they then should lie on the floor on their backs with heads pointing toward the center of the circle. Each student should now have a sense of his or her own personal space. With only the ceiling in their line of vision, they should be able to concentrate on hearing

the music and responding with body movements. Following are some adaptations for activities based on students' abilities:

Stand in a circle facing outward.

Sit in a circle facing outward.

Stand or sit in different parts of the room, all facing away from the center of the room.

2. Play your choice of African music. When you call out the name of a body part, students will move that isolated part to the music.

Free Dance to African Music

This free dance activity is quite effective following the isolated body parts warm-up to African music. However, if you do it on a separate day or out of context, make sure a general warm-up is done first. Use as many or few of these steps as are applicable to your students' abilities.

Directions

1. Have students stand (or sit if standing is not possible) in a circle, facing the center. Leave adequate space for movement between them. Students may also find their own space in the open area of a classroom or gymnasium.

2. Ask them to pretend they are very heavy. How does it make their feet feel? Can they feel their feet pressing into the ground? Tell them to take a few steps toward the center and back again and feel as though their feet are connecting them to the earth. This is what the feet on the ground means to African dancers: a connection with the earth.

3. You may do an exploration with your students in which they hold the head as still as possible and try moving the arms, the shoulders, and other body parts without moving the head. In African dance, the head serves as a balancing point for the whole body.

4. Turn on the African music of your choice.

5. Have students move to the music and rhythms they hear, using their bodies any way they wish. They may move around the circle or in any free space available. Remind them of different body parts and different rhythms. Look for free response and expression to the music.

6. Remind them that African dancers make up their own movements much of the time.

7. Compliment and reinforce their creative movement contributions.

Circle Dance to African Music

This circle dance lets students experience the communal and spectator aspects of African dance. They will also experience trying to keep a steady beat with a simple repeated motion and have a chance to free dance to the music as a soloist.

1. Have students stand (or sit) in a large circle, facing the center.

2. Model, or have a student create, a simple movement. If it has an accompanying sound, like a clap or a slap, so much the better.

3. Have everyone try the movement. See if everyone can do it together in unison. You can say "1, 2, ready, go" and do it on the number 1 of a "1, 2, 3, 4" count. If this is a problem, just have students attempt to make this movement even once together.

4. Put on the African music of your choice. Have students come together in a circle.

5. If the class or part of the class can keep a beat by making the one simple movement (and possibly sound), have them do it to the music. If the music can be counted to in four, count "1, 2, 3, 4" and try to make the movement on count 1, repeating the counting cycle.

6. While you or others in the class keep a "movement beat," have one student go to the center and free dance to the music. You or that student can decide when he or she returns to the circle and the next person goes to the center and dances. The circle should have a supportive and enthusiastic feeling that encourages the person making up the solo in the center of the circle. Go around the circle, one person at a time, taking turns being the solo dancer.

7. If students are higher functioning, less inhibited, and having fun, the solo dancer can dance over to anyone in the circle and have that person become the new dancer in the center.

8. The solo dancer may also dance over to someone in the circle and "invite" him or her (with movements only) to join the solo dancer in the center. The two dancers can then perform free dance in the circle.

Circle Dance: Call and Response

Make sure you do a warm-up if you are starting with this activity. (**Note:** *In African music the response can be different than the call.*)

Directions

1. Stand in a circle, facing the center.

2. Without music, make one movement or a short series of repetitive movements, like two arm raises or three nods. The movement you make will be determined by what your students can do physically. Have students try to replicate your movement.

3. The call movement should be accompanied by a vocal sound, or make up a chant that goes with the movement. Do it once alone and tell students that this is the call. When they repeat it back to you in unison, that is the response.

4. After using more movements and having students replicate them, explain that this movement and sound dialogue between leader and group is called "call and response" in African music.

5. Turn on the music and lead the class in this African version of what could almost be "Simon Says." You may choose other student leaders to make the "call."

Partner Dances with African Music

Directions

1. Have students stand in a circle or other formation that is conducive to working with a partner.

2. Make sure each person has a partner. Explain that the partners will talk back and forth to each other, taking turns, one at a time. Tell students that instead of talking with words, each person will "talk" with movements.

3. Put on your chosen music. Decide, in each group of two, which partner will move first. That person will move to the music until you give a signal (such as a clap of a

hand or a hit on a drum) to change who is "talking." If the children are higher functioning, you may exchange their parts every four or eight beats. You may count beats softly aloud, or if counting is a problem while attending the children, simply say "change" when the time seems appropriate.

Other Ideas

In some African dances, movements are also derived from everyday activities such as planting, harvesting, carrying water or gourds on the head or shoulders, and so forth. Depending on your students' abilities, you can explore everyday life as part of a study in African culture. Have students make up movements from sweeping, planting, or other daily activities. Change them into repetitive dance movements and integrate some of these movements into the dance activities above. Dancing or creating movement activities to music from various cultures is one of the most vital and exciting ways to begin to learn about the traditions and sensibilities of those cultures.

Chinese Red Silk Dance

One of the most visually striking dances of ancient China was the "Red Silk" or "Red Ribbon" dance. Dancers would attach yards and yards of red silk "ribbon" (actually, the width of a wide sash) to the ends of slender wooden sticks. Holding the sticks in one or both hands, waving their arms, and moving their bodies, the dancers would create beautiful red waves, circles, spirals, and figure-eights in the air above, below, and around their bodies. When at rest, dancers would gather the red silk at the end of the stick to look like an enormous red rose. Even today, centuries later, this traditional dance is performed at Chinese dance and music festivals throughout the world.

If you and your students are studying China or Asia, or if visual stimulus and simple upper body movement are important, together you can create your own version of the Red Silk Dance.

Activity Process

> *Estimated Time:* Two sessions, one to create the red silk "ribbons" and one to create the dance.
>
> *Suggested Music:* See "Chinese Music" on page 37.

Level

Low to high functioning students. Minimum physical ability to move arms, if not legs, and to hold a light object in the hand(s) while moving the arms.

Benefits

- Fine and gross motor coordination
- Cognition of the relationship between physical movement and the creation of visual forms in space
- Musical and cultural awareness
- Exploration of space in and around the body on low, medium, and high levels

Materials

- Tape of Chinese music
- Lightweight wood chopsticks

- Red crepe paper streamers cut in appropriate lengths according to the size and coordination of students (or narrow lengths of lightweight red fabric or ribbon)
- Glue, tape, etc.
- Blunt-tipped scissors

Session 1

1. You and your aides can prepare the red silk ribbons ahead of time by attaching the red streamers or fabric to the ends of the chopsticks with glue, tape, or whatever works best for you. If you do this ahead of time, children will be able to use them to dance immediately.

2. If your students have the ability to help make their own streamers, you and your aides can assist them in doing so. Chinese music in the background not only sets the mood but prepares students for the type of music they will hear in the movement activity.

3. Set red streamers aside to dry.

Session 2

This is essentially a free dance session to Chinese music. Students will experiment with movements that use the red streamers to create beautiful and different shapes in the surrounding air space. One arm only may be used, or arms and body movements. In creating their red air shapes, encourage students to explore:

- Big and small, or long and short movements
- Circular or spiral movements
- Fast and slow
- Figure-eight movements
- Smooth and jerky movements
- Zigzags
- High and low
- Arcs or waves
- Spaces all around their bodies

This activity is so much fun to do and to perceive visually, you can do it again in follow-up sessions with different kinds of music. Note if and how different types of music affect students' movements and the air shapes they create.

Variation

If students are higher functioning and want to create a "real" choreographed dance, they should decide on three or four favorite movements. Call the movements **A**, **B**, **C**, and **D**. For **ABA** and "rondo" form dances, see "What Makes a Dance" on page 2.

A Dance "For the Seasons"

This variation on the Chinese Red Silk Dance will lend itself to interactive collaboration if your students are able to work in small groups with adult supervision. Children will use similar techniques as in the previous activity to make simple props that represent something in nature. Using these props, children create dances that honor each season.

The final dance will have four sections, one to represent each season. Students in each group will create a dance for one of the seasons. Although the pressure on each group is relatively minimal, the final dance will have a more complex form when assembled together.

Activity Process

Estimated Time: Two to three sessions, one session for making props and one to two sessions for the dance.

Suggested Music: The Four Seasons. This piece was written by Antonio Vivaldi and published in 1725 for violin solo and string orchestra. Each movement represents one of the seasons. You may want to tape the first 5–10 minutes of each movement, or the entire movements for longer rehearsal purposes, on a separate tape. Most likely the final performance of each season will be shorter than the true length of each movement, so you will need to decide on a stopping point in the music.

Level

Low to high functioning students. Minimum physical ability to move arms, if not legs, and to hold a light object in the hand(s) while moving the arms.

Benefits

- Fine and gross motor coordination
- Cognition of the relationship between physical movement and the creation of visual forms in space
- Awareness of the seasons and characteristics of each one
- Exploration of space in and around the body on low, medium, and high levels

Warm-Up Session

1. Draw pictures of the seasons. Post the pictures of the seasons in groups of spring, summer, winter, and fall around the classroom.

2. Discuss what happens in nature in each of the seasons: "What is the weather like? How do you feel? What colors do you associate with each season?"

Vivaldi's music is descriptive in the timbres (sound colors) and movements of the sound. As in previous activities, it may be a good idea to work through movement ideas before finalizing them to the music.

Materials

- Tape or tapes of Vivaldi's *The Four Seasons*
- Lightweight wood chopsticks
- Crepe paper streamers in all colors: pink, purple, red, green, blue, white, etc.
- Glue, tape, etc.
- Scissors

Session 1

1. Divide the class into four groups. (If you cannot work in four small groups, try adapting the process to working as a class.)

2. Assign each group a season or write the four seasons on four slips of paper, put the slips in a container, hat, box, etc., and have group leaders pick their season.

3. Each group should then pick one image from nature from their season (if children are on a higher functioning level, they may pick two images). Examples:

   Spring: *flowers*
   Summer: *trees*
   Fall: *brightly colored leaves*
   Winter: *snow*

4. Each group should then pick one or two colors that they associate with their season. Examples:

   Flowers: *pink and purple*
   Trees: *green and brown*
   Leaves: *orange and yellow*
   Snow: *white and gray*

5. Have students in each group create or cut their own crepe paper, ribbon, or fabric streamers as described previously. This time, each group will choose colors, based on their images. The length of the streamers may be shorter or longer than the red steamers since they will be representing flowers, leaves, and snow. Play Vivaldi's *Four Seasons* in the background as the children work.

6. After the streamers are complete, set them aside to dry.

Session 2

1. Without props or music, review the nature image each group has chosen.

2. Choose one or two movement ideas that are inspired by the image. If the image is snow, discuss how snow can fall gently, or violently as in a storm. Have children create movements with their hands and arms of snow falling gently. Movements inspired by the image of gently falling snow in a snowstorm could be called floating movements.

3. Explore all the possibilities of each movement. Do not have children "be" the snow. Encourage them to explore all the different ways they can float their arms, hands, and bodies. Have them float high and low, fast and slow, side to side, etc.

4. After children have thoroughly explored their movements (not necessarily the image), have them re-explore the movements using their streamer props.

5. Have students focus on the movements they've created (rather than the original image) and how they might vary or change them to make them interesting:

   Big and small movements
   High and low movements
   Back and forth or side to side movements
   Circular movements
   Sharp, angular or zigzag movements
   Movements that involve the whole body in addition to arms and hands

6. Decide whether your group dance will move through space. If you move through space, will you walk? Run? Skip?

7. Decide on two or three favorite movement ideas. Call them **A**, **B**, and **C**.

8. Arrange these ideas into a simple sequence such as **ABA**, **ABC**, or **ABACA**, any other arrangements, as described before. The ideas and sequence of ideas should reflect your students' abilities. This simple sequence is basically your dance.

9. After students have their movement sequence memorized (if this is possible), have each group practice to music. If any group's dance is too short, it can be repeated once or twice.

10. Make any movement changes the music might inspire.

11. When you are ready to perform, start with spring and have each group do their dance "For the Seasons" in sequence to the appropriate movement of Vivaldi's composition.

Note: Although Vivaldi's music is very descriptive and motivating to work with, by working through movement ideas first without music, children can concentrate solely on movement. Adding the music later provides a wonderful "musical glue" for the sequence of movements of your final dance. This dance could be perfected enough to be performed before an audience. Each group is highlighted without bearing the responsibility for all four seasons. The colorful props add visual interest and the music is a well-known masterpiece. The theme of the seasons is adaptable to various occasions and is also an effective learning vehicle. Your own creativity and your students' abilities, as usual, will define the length and complexity of your final dance.

Music for Different Modes of Locomotion

Walking

1. Johannes Brahms, Piano Quartet no. 1, op. 25 VI, Andante Con Moto
2. Johann Sebastian Bach, Prelude in C Major, no. 1 from Book I of *Well-Tempered Clavier*
3. Wolfgang Amadeus Mozart, Symphony no. 40 in G Minor, K-550, Movement I Molto Allegro
4. Maurice Ravel, *Bolero*
5. Erik Satie, Solo Piano Music
6. Johann Sebastian Bach, *Goldberg Variations*
7. Wolfgang Amadeus Mozart, Symphony no. 41, "Jupiter," K.551

Running

1. Edward Elgar, *Variations on an Original Theme,* op.36, "Enigma," Variation VII (Troyte)
2. Serge Prokofiev, IV "Troika" from *Lieutenant Kije Suite*
3. Igor Stravinsky, *The Firebird IV,* "Infernal Dance"

Skipping

1. Ludwig van Beethoven, Symphony no. 7 in A, op. 92, Movement I, Vivace
2. Frederic Chopin, Waltz in E Flat, op. 18
3. Franz Liszt, *Mephisto Waltz* no. 1

Jumping

1. Antonin Dvorak, *Slavonic Dances*
2. Maurice Ravel, *Rhapsodie Espagnole*
3. Serge Prokofiev, *Romeo and Juliet,* Suite I, "Folk Dance"

Sliding

1. Sainte Colombe, Concerto XLII: Dalain, Movement I, "Dalain"
2. Béla Bartók, Concerto for Orchestra, Movement II, Givco delle Coppie
3. Bedrich Smetana, *Die Moldau* (Vitara)

Floating

1. Eric Satie, *Gymnopedie* no. 1
2. Edvard Grieg, "Morning Mood," from *Peer Gynt Suite,* op. 55, 46
3. John Cage, *Dream*

Leaping

1. Ludwig van Beethoven, Concerto for Piano and Orchestra no. 5 in E Flat Major, op. 73
3. Felix Mendelssohn, *A Midsummer Night's Dream,* Scherzo
3. Ludwig van Beethoven, Symphony no. 9, Movement II, Scherzo

Music That Suggests Images

1. Nicolai Rimsky-Korsakov, *Scheherazade Suite* op. 35
2. Claude Debussy, *La Mer*
3. Hector Berlioz, *Symphonie Fantastique* op. 14
4. Modest Mussorgsky, *Night on Bald Mountain*

Music for Movement

1. Johannes Pachelbel, *Canon in D*
2. Peter Ilitch Tchaikovsky, *Serenade for Strings in C,* op. 48, no. 2, Waltz
3. Antonin Dvorak, *Slavonic Dances*
4. Wolfgang Amadeus Mozart, Symphony no. 40 in G Minor, K.550

Music for Calmness

1. Erik Satie, Solo Piano Music Including *Gymnopedie* no. 1, 2, 3
2. Frederic Chopin, *Nocturnes*
3. Sieur de Sainte-Colombe, *Concerts à Deux Violes Esgales*
4. Johann Sebastian Bach, Complete Solo Cello Suites

Music for Positive Stimulation

1. Edward Elgar, *Variations on an Original Theme* op. 36, "Enigma"
2. Antonio Vivaldi, *The Four Seasons*
3. Wolfgang Amadeus Mozart, Piano Sonatas
4. Felix Mendelssohn, Symphony no. 4 in A Major op. 90, "Italian" Movement I, Allegro Vivace

5. Johannes Brahms, Symphony no. 4 in E Minor op. 98, Movement III, Allegro Giocoso Poco Meno Presto

6. Zoltan Kodaly II, "Viennese Musical Clock" from *"Harry Janos" Suite*

African Dance Music

1. Babatunde Olatunji, *Drums of Passion: Rykodisc RCD10107 The Beat*

2. Babatunde Olatunji, *Drums of Passion: Rykodisc RCD10102 The Invocation*

3. Various Artists, *African Songs and Rhythms for Children,* Folkways/Smithsonian, 45011

Chinese Music

1. The Chinese Music Ensemble of New York, *Beloved Chinese Folksongs*, Chesky Records, W0121

2. The Guo Brothers + Yuan, *Real World Carol,* 2310 Shung Tian

3. Lam Sik-Kwan, *Flowing Chinese Sunrise,* 8523 Flutes Imported by Qualiton

4. Other Chinese music in general

Music for the Activity "For the Seasons"

1. Antonio Vivaldi, *The Four Seasons* op. 8, nos. 1–4

Refer to "Visual Arts Music Appendix" (page 153) for more music suggestions from different genres.

ABA. A three-part form in dance or music using two basic ideas, **A** and **B**. The **A** idea provides unity and cohesiveness to the form and the **B** idea provides contrast.

ABACADA. A form of dance or music composition called "rondo." This "rondo" can use three or more movement ideas, such as **A**, **B**, **C**, and **D**. Those ideas can be arranged so that **A** provides a returning unity and **B**, **C**, and **D** provide contrast.

Action. A movement event.

Call and response. A form of music or dance activity common in African and other cultures where a leader makes a solo "call" in movement and/or sound and a group responds to the call either in exact imitation or with a different "answer."

Choreographer. A person who makes up dances.

Duet. A dance for two people or two people dancing together.

Elevation. A movement in which the body is propelled off the ground and into the air, as with a leap, a jump or a hop.

Folk dance or traditional dance. Dances that have grown out of specific traditions or cultures and are usually performed by the group of people who created them. These dances are usually communal and not originally created to be performed on a stage. The movements of these dances generally are passed from one generation to the next.

Form. The plan or organization of smaller movement ideas into a larger design that has a beginning, middle, and end of some sort. Form uses different ideas, such as might be labeled idea **A**, idea **B**, or idea **C**, in various combinations.

Improvisation. Spontaneously created movement. Simultaneous choreography and performance.

Kinesthetic. Refers to the ability of the sensory organs in the body's muscles, tendons, and joints to respond and relate to the stimulus of watching or performing a dance.

Levels. Refers to high, medium, or low spatial heights of movement.

Locomotion. Movement that takes the body from one place to another.

Movement theme. A movement idea or tightly ordered cohesive series of movement ideas that are used as main and often recurring events in a dance. Themes can be developed, varied, and recur to create unity. Secondary themes that differ from the main theme can create contrast.

Narrative dance. A choreographed dance that follows a story line and/or tells a story.

Pattern. An organized sequence or series of shorter movement ideas that meld into a larger, more complex entity that can be repeated, if desired.

Personal space. All planes, levels, and directions of space near and farther away from the body's center. It also includes the space or kinesphere that one's body occupies.

Polyrhythm. Many different rhythms occurring simultaneously.

Solo. A dance for one person, or one person dancing alone.

Trio. A dance for three people, or three people dancing together.

Unison. Everyone doing exactly the same movement at exactly the same time.

Dance Bibliography

Chernoff, John Miller. *African Rhythm and African Sensibility.* Chicago and London: University of Chicago Press, 1979.

Hutchinson, Ann. *Labanotation (The System of Analyzing and Recording Movement).* 3d ed., rev. New York: Theatre Arts Books, 1977.

Joyce, Mary. *First Steps in Teaching Creative Dance to Children.* 3d ed. Mountain View, Calif.: Mayfield Publishing, 1994.

Laban, Rudolf. *Laban's Principles of Dance and Movement Notation.* 2d ed. Boston: Plays, Inc., 1975.

Levete, Gina. *No Handicap to Dance.* London: Souvenir Press Ltd., 1987, 1993.

Martin, John. *The Dance in Theory.* Princeton, N.J.: Princeton Book Company Publishers, 1965.

Warren, Bernie, ed. *Using the Creative Arts in Therapy: A Practical Introduction.* 2d ed. New York: Routledge, 1993.

CHAPTER TWO

Drama

Art is the lie that reveals the truth.

—Picasso

Nowhere is that truth more concretely accessible than in drama. If we understand the truth in a dramatic moment and empathize with what the characters are feeling, we have experienced insight, even though the outer trappings are fantasy.

Our roles in life change constantly. We are influenced by our hopes and dreams, circumstances and relationships. Theater deals with relationships with one another and the world around us more directly than any other art form. The meaning of our words comes not only from what we say but how we say it. The art of drama is the art of human interaction and communication, during which we confront conflicts and discover resolutions. In the ever-changing circumstances of our lives and in the roles we play every day, we find the essence of drama.

The origins of drama lie in storytelling. From the storyteller's imagination spring time, place, character, and circumstance. When real people embody improvised characters and live out those situations, stories become theater.

A storyteller must become both the narrator and the characters to help the listener understand the action that propels the story line. Drama must have action and reaction—even if it is a single actor addressing a question to an unanswering audience.

Drama and the Student with Disabilities

Using the basic elements of drama, students with disabilities have the potential to develop practical life skills and experience profound personal growth. When a special needs student "inhabits someone else's skin" for a period of time, that child experiences empathy and a great sense of personal freedom in which parts of the self can be explored through the eyes of another. In this endeavor the imagination is key. When role-playing, the child is given an opportunity to discharge emotion safely and appropriately. He or she can learn to exercise emotional discipline and judgment. Boundaries can be established and respected. In the process, the child achieves a greater understanding of what other human beings feel and why.

The art of theater is tremendously flexible, which helps in adapting activities to different levels of ability. All children, not just special students, learn through their senses. For some students, not only may the physical, intellectual, or emotional development be impaired or delayed, but some of the senses as well.

Theater works extremely well for people with hearing impairments or those who are deaf. They can see and respond to facial expressions and body language and use their own symbol system to communicate. Activities and scenarios can be designed or adapted to use those senses and abilities that are the strongest and to challenge, gently, those areas that need to be exercised. The child must communicate through the use of language and gesture. With the senses, emotions, mind, and body activated in an integrated way, powerful kinesthetic learning can occur.

It has been said that everything in this world is created twice: once in the imagination and again in physical reality. If this is true, when working with drama a child is given, first, the chance to envision states of being, feeling, and doing, and second, the opportunity to make these imagined states a reality. This they can do first in the safety of the classroom and perhaps later in the real world.

Life Skills Through Drama

To express ourselves, we must be able to communicate by speaking and, if possible, by using our faces and bodies to amplify that expression. We must be able to focus on and listen to what someone is saying to react and respond in an appropriate manner.

Many of the games and play exercises in drama provide an array of opportunities for developing listening skills. To play a game, directions must be listened to and understood. Before a story can be transformed into a play and acted out, children must be able to listen to the story, understand the story line, and learn who the characters are and what actions they will be performing.

In dramatic interaction between two or more students, the children must listen to each other. Eye contact, often a problem with some special students, can be reinforced. Interpreting facial expressions and body language and listening to tone of voice also helps students understand and decode what is being communicated.

Like other art forms, drama can encourage and motivate speaking, attention, concentration, self-esteem, and a multitude of other cognitive and interpersonal skills. The process of creative problem solving in drama can be as simple as how to greet someone, as multi-tasked as buying a ticket to attend a movie, or as involved as applying for a job. Through working in drama, children can first be helped to visualize what needs to be done, then practice doing it within the safe boundaries of the classroom.

The Audience

From the very beginning, students should be made aware that the audience is a vital part of any dramatic activity, from creative games to a finished play. Although perceiving and being perceived is part of any interaction in drama, the audience mirrors this perception and amplifies the experience by seeing the entire interactive process from a unique perspective.

The performing arts involve three components of the creative experience: the creator of the artwork; the performers or persons who make that creative idea a physical reality; and the perceivers, who look, listen, and appreciate the results. In improvised or spontaneous creation, the first two roles combine much as they do in the visual arts.

The audience is the silent participant in all the dramatic activities of games and role-playing. If an actor is alone on stage, the audience can be the other presence to whom that actor speaks or addresses a question, such as in a monologue.

Your children should understand the ground rules from the start. As members of the audience, their role is as important as that of an actor. Their active participation in observing actually enhances all that is happening. Knowing this, they will become a vital part of the creative experience. In this process, focusing and concentration skills are strengthened and developed.

Coaching Your Students

In drama activities, your role might be likened to that of a director. Some of a director's responsibilities are to help actors interpret and deliver lines, decide where they will stand, and tell them how and when to move. As director, you will coach and cue your students. However, one of your most important functions will be to encourage your students to stay focused on the dramatic activity even though words or sequences of events might be momentarily forgotten.

Establish from the beginning that you will be calling out directions as part of the entire process in your drama activities. Tell students that your calling directions to them is not a signal to stop. They should continue to do what they are doing while listening to your instructions. You may call students by their real names or their characters' names depending on each child and the situation. This kind of support will help children stay focused. Knowing that you are there for them will also increase their courage and confidence.

 ## Fantasy versus Reality

There are some students with disabilities for whom the boundaries between fantasy and reality are blurred in real life. There are others who may become confused by this distinction in drama activities even if this is not normally a problem for them. Many special students eagerly adapt to fanciful situations. There are others who may appear to be doing this, but the scenario has become a reality in their minds. Stay aware and watchful of the distinction between children who are positively engaged in the successful use of their imaginations and those for whom a fantasy situation has become a reality. If a child continues in the same emotional state when the exercise or game has stopped, he or she may have accepted the conditions of the game as reality. If this is the case, you may have to take that child aside and explain that the game is make-believe and is only "real" in the imagination. Sometimes using a clear sounding bell or other distinctive sound can signal when the magic period of theater begins and when it ends, at which time everyone goes back to everyday life.

 ## Play

Children go through several stages in their ability to play. Initially, children play alone, even though they may be in the presence of other children. At ages three or four, children begin to talk to each other and share toys, even playing the same game at the same time. By ages four or five, they will have developed enough skills to interact with other children, sharing fantasies and being able to play the same game together with more complex interaction. Because your children operate on levels that are not necessarily "in sync" with their chronological age, you must design and adapt your activities accordingly.

 ## Theater Games

Games are a more structured form of play that allows the player to experiment with new ways of being and acting while in a safe environment. Both games and play utilize the freedom of imagination in transforming people, places, objects, and occurrences. Games are generally thought of as activities defined by a set of rules. In sports, those rules are very specific. Since most theater games involve improvisation, the rule may be nothing more than a collective agreement about location, character, and circumstance.

Most games require a leader to provide structure. As the leader, you will guide the action. Remember that some of the best learning in life is accomplished by imitation. When playing theater games, children will, at times, imitate and model each other.

Games are wonderful warm-ups for more involved theater activities such as play writing, rehearsing scenes from a play, or acting out a story. Using your imagination, any game format can be adapted to suit your educational goals and your students' abilities.

Drama Activities

 ## Theater Games and Warm-Ups

The following activities use the idea of play within the context of a game format. Most of these exercises involve group interaction in some form or another. Students must be adaptable and responsive in a variety of ways.

All of these games can be changed and adapted as far as subject matter is concerned. They can also be simplified for lower functioning students.

Fruit Salad

Activity Process

> *Estimated Time:* One session or less
>
> *Suggested Music:* Optional, or none

This game requires the students to use their bodies, as well as the skills of listening and being attentive to respond appropriately. This game usually results in an atmosphere charged with fun and anticipation. Regardless of the adaptations you may choose to make, it is the excitement and motivation of playing that serves most as a warm-up for any ensuing theater activities. When the activity is first being learned, it might take a full session. Later, as the process becomes more familiar, it can be used for a shorter time as a warm-up.

Level

Although the subject matter has great flexibility, there is a requirement that students be able to get up and move from one chair to another in a circle format. Adapt the game to the abilities of students who can function on a higher level physically than intellectually.

Benefits

- Motivates recognition of fruits or vegetables, numbers, colors, words, geometric shapes, or other objects or conceptual classifications
- Motivates movement through space with a specific goal in mind
- Encourages involvement and participation
- Facilitates cognition and reinforces learning in a variety of areas
- Exercises and develops body, voice, intellect, emotions, and the ability to interact with others

This activity is a variation on the old game of musical chairs. Directions for the first version of the game, "Fruit Salad," are given. However, it is in the teacher's adaptations that the real creative challenges and benefits of this activity become evident.

44

Directions

1. Have students arrange chairs in a circle, with each student and yourself sitting in a chair facing the center.

2. After everyone is seated, take one chair away (it could be your own).

3. Now there is one less chair than there are people. It may be a good idea to start with yourself being the person without a seat. To begin the game, stand in the center of the circle and ask students to name four different fruits. (Two or three might be more appropriate in some cases.)

4. Go around the circle and assign each person the name of a fruit that was named, in the order they were called out. Repeat the cycle of giving students the four fruit names until every student has a fruit name.

5. Check that all students remember what fruit name they have. Then, for example, ask all the apples to raise their hands when you call out "apples." Do the same with the other three fruit.

6. When you are satisfied that all are clear about what fruit they are, explain that the person in the center (you can do this first) will call out the name of one fruit, such as "bananas." When bananas are called, all the banana people must jump up and change chairs. This includes the person in the center. Since there is one less chair than there are people vying for seats, someone will end up without a chair. That person will then stand in the center of the circle, and when everyone is settled, will call out the name of one of the four fruits. Those people will then hurry to exchange chairs, while the person in the middle also tries to get one of the empty seats.

7. Each student who loses a seat is compensated by standing in the center and "leading" the next phase of the activity by choosing the name of the fruit to call. However, explain to students that if the person in the center wants to, he or she can call out "fruit salad," and everyone in the circle must jump up and change seats. This adds an extra dimension of excitement and anticipation to the game.

Two rules that you might want to mention follow:

• Everyone must go to a *different* chair when the name of their fruit is called.

• No bodily contact should occur in the process of trying to get to a chair.

Variations and Adaptations

If students' cognitive levels are low, you may want to review the fruits and their names before playing the game. Bring in an apple, banana, orange, and grapes for the students to see. If they need more help remembering what fruit name they are, you could give each student a specific fruit to hold. The person in the center could pick up one of the four fruits laid in the center of the circle. If the leader picks up an apple and says "apple," everyone holding an apple would get up and scramble for a different chair.

This adaptation could also be done with cards that have the name or picture representations of the fruits printed on them. Cards could be hung around students' necks with soft yarn. Colored ribbons could be tied on students' arms (for the "color" activity below) to facilitate unencumbered movement.

If you are working to identify numbers, this game can easily be adapted to assigning numbers to students. You could also substitute dots for numbers. For example, if you want the "number 3" people to get up and scramble for chairs, you could hold up a large card with three clear dots or symbols on it. This way, students would have to count to know the card was calling the "3" people. Likewise, if you are practicing reading skills, the word "three" could be shown on a card.

If you are trying to develop color identification skills, you may go through similar adaptations, depending on the level of your students' abilities. Red may be indicated by the person in the center by saying "red," showing a sheet of paper that is red, or holding up a card with the word "red" written on it. When you want everyone to jump up and go for chairs, you could call out the word "rainbow!"

Categories of vegetables could be dealt with in the same manner as the previous adaptations using spoken words or cards with pictures or printed words. Real vegetables could be used to concretize things further for lower functioning students. When the leader wants everyone to run for chairs, he or she could call out "mixed vegetables!"

With animals, the same could be done using different animal names or even categories of animals such as mammals or reptiles. When everyone is to run for chairs, the leader in the middle of the circle could call out "zoo!" If you are studying geometric shapes, circles, squares, rectangles, and triangles, cards, colors, or objects could be used as in the other adaptations.

Musical instruments can be dealt with in a similar fashion, with the cue word for everyone to get up being "orchestra!" If you are studying language, you can create a structure that uses verbs and nouns and have appropriate calls made from the center of the circle. For example, if some people have words like "tree," "car," or "table," and some have words like "run," "walk," or "laugh," when "noun" is called, the "tree," "car," and "table" people would scramble to a new seat. "Dictionary!" or some other appropriate cue word could be used to signal everyone to get up. The possibilities are endless.

These adaptations are suggestions that can be refined and modified according to what you are studying, the approach you are stressing, the number of students you have, their level of ability, and the drama activity, if any, that will follow this warm-up game.

Mirrors

Activity Process

Estimated Time: One session or less

Suggested Music: Music is optional, but recommended after directions are understood. If used, it should be something slow and not distracting.

"Mirrors" is a well known theater game that uses the basic idea of imitation to promote concentration, precision, and interpersonal sensitivity. Through the mirror game, students can explore physical gestures alone or in combination with particular emotions. *When beginning the mirror activity with your students, it is a good idea for you to start by leading it yourself.*

Level

Students must have adequate vision to see the gestures and facial expressions of the person they are to mirror. They should be able to imitate the physical gestures of the leader. The gestures, in turn, may be adapted to the physical abilities of the students. Whether or not a student can recognize and experience emotion in this activity is less measurable. Therefore if, in the second stage of the exercise, an emotion is combined with a physical gesture, certain students will at least be able to participate in the gesture even if they do not perceive the emotion being projected, or vice versa.

Benefits

- Physical discipline
- Ability to focus on the task of perceiving visually and replicating physically
- Ability to perceive emotion in another through gesture or facial expression
- Working cooperatively
- Ability to empathize with other human beings and be "in their shoes"

Directions

1. Stand where students can see you clearly. If students cannot stand, they may sit.

2. Explain that you are going to pretend you are looking in a mirror. (You may want to have an actual mirror on hand to demonstrate.) The students (the entire class) are your mirror. For every single move you make, the "mirror" will make it back to you as closely as possible and at the same time you are doing it.

3. Begin with something simple. All your movements should be extremely clear and executed slowly. You might start with something as simple as raising your right arm and lowering it. This is also a good time to clarify to the class which arm they should be raising so that there is no confusion. If you raise your right arm, they will raise their left arms.

4. Following are some simple gestures you might start with. These are shapes in space that have no extra connotation in terms of meaning or emotion. They are simply to begin the process of concentration and gestural replication. Each gesture can be repeated more than once. Feel free to add your own movements to this list.

   Slowly raise your right arm and lower it.

   Slowly raise your left arm and lower it.

   Slowly raise both arms together and lower them.

   Turn your head to the right. Turn your head to the left.

   Look up, tilting your head back.

   Look down, tilting your head forward.

   Dip at the knees and raise back up.

5. If this is successful, you may want to expand to gestures that have connotative meanings and combine those with emotions that can also be shown with facial expressions. Before doing this, however, you may want to isolate each emotion and facial expression and practice only that with your students, holding the rest of the body still.

   Facial expressions and emotions to mirror include

   a big smile (happy);

   a big frown (angry or very sad);

   a sad expression (sad);

   a mild smile (mildly happy);

   having your mouth open and eyes wide (scared); and

   laughing, sleeping, or others students can make up.

   While you are making the facial expressions, look around at the students and see how they are doing. Some students may be genuinely feeling the emotion you are projecting yet be unable to mirror your facial expression. Others may have no trouble mirroring your expression but be oblivious to the emotion behind it and treat that exercise as just a physical game.

6. The next step is to choose gestures that have emotions to go with them. Explain to students that they are to imitate your physical gestures and facial expressions and that their challenge is also to feel the emotions you are feeling and "send them back" to you. Toward this end, it might be a good idea to go over every gesture and emotion first with your students:

Wave hello and smile (happy—glad to see someone). You might do this gesture and ask a student to make up a story of who or what he or she sees. Have the student tell the class who he or she is.

Wave goodbye (sad—sorry to say goodbye).

Shrug your shoulders (puzzled—not knowing something).

Cross your arms, tap your foot, frown (impatient, waiting).

Stand with hands on hips, frowning (angry).

Shake your hands or arms, using a frightened expression (scared).

7. You can go through one, two, three, or more of these at a time, talking through what the children perceive as the meaning of the gesture and the emotion registered in the body movement and facial expression. Then, depending on how many you feel your students can handle, go slowly, without speaking, through each of the gestures and emotions you have previewed with them. Continue waving hello with a smile, for example, until you see everyone doing the same gesture and, hopefully, understanding, experiencing, and even projecting the same feeling.

8. Continuing in a slow and clear manner, with no verbal directions if possible, go through the other suggested gestures and emotions, adding any ideas of your own to the list. Watch the class carefully. Stay with one gesture and emotion until everyone has had a chance to experience it. Make your transitions to another gesture and emotion slow and clear.

9. If you feel a student is capable of leading, you may choose a student leader for other sessions.

Progressions and Adaptations

Gestures and Roles

In preparation for other activities, you may want to explore what someone does in a certain job or activity through the mirror game. If one of your future activities will be to improvise a scene in which someone is collecting tickets at a movie theater, the leader could assume the role of the ticket taker and create a simple, repetitive gesture that everyone else copies. Everything should be done in slow motion. Following are some other suggestions for gestural movements based on character roles that could be used in an extended mirror activity:

- Shooting a basket or hitting a softball,
- Hoeing a garden,
- Selling a hot dog,
- Diving and swimming,
- Driving a car,
- Holding and rocking a baby, and
- Picking berries.

Games can also be created in which students must guess and identify what kind of activity a person might be performing with each gesture.

Partners and Mirroring

If your students are capable of working in pairs, this is a silent activity that allows partners to work independently in the same room, at the same time, with no sound disruption.

Have students pair off and take turns being the leader in their own mirror activity. Aides can work with different pairs of students. The gestures need not have emotions attached to them and can be purely physical and improvised. It is good to do this after the class has successfully followed your lead in the group mirror activity, so that you know they understand the process. Remind them to move slowly and silently.

When students have worked in pairs, tell them they can practice again to prepare to do their mirror activity in front of the class. The idea is to be so in tune with each other that the class cannot tell which person is the leader and which is the follower. The students may then practice again and take turns "performing" their mirroring exercises for the class.

Obviously, to participate in this extension of the mirror activity, students will have to have an appropriate degree of independence and understanding of the process. But the value of this process is as much in the perception of others performing the same task as it is in performing and being observed.

Creating Imaginary Objects

This is a wonderful group activity that stretches the imagination of both the participants and the observers. A small group of students (from four to eight) will be asked to create collectively something like a tree, a chair, a car, or a flower.

For mainstream students, the process of the imagination can be very similar to that of some special students. However, the difference is that mainstream students might be able to recognize quickly that a tree has roots, a trunk, branches, and leaves. Some special students may need help in the initial analysis of the components of a specific object they will have to create. Therefore, to get to the point where their imaginations can take over, it is up to you to make sure their understanding of the task and the object is clear. In this process, students can learn parts of an object through their physicalization of a given part.

One value of these games is audience observation. This not only reinforces the importance of audience in a theatrical context but acclimates the "actors" to the idea of being observed. What is "performed" is very interesting to watch, so those students who are not *playing* actively can be involved by actively *observing*.

Activity Process

Estimated Time: One session

Suggested Music: No music

Level

Students should be at a learning level to be able to perceive, for example, what a chair is, and that it has four legs, a seat, and a back. The students' abstract cognitive skills must be such that they can project themselves into a structure of human bodies and perform their "role" as the leg of a chair. There are some students who can comprehend the idea and process and even perform their function in the role of something like the leg of a chair but will need assistance and support in getting into the position of that role both physically and psychologically. Once there, however, those students can have the perspective of how their part fits into creating the entire idea of an imaginary chair.

Benefits

- Working in a collaborative group process
- Abstract thinking skills

- Imagination and improvisation
- Synthesis and review of information from other areas of study

Directions

1. Choose four students and tell them that their challenge is to create a chair using their bodies. (Objects to be created may be picked from a hat by the leader of the group.)

2. Depending on the students' level of abilities, they may be able to work alone in front of the class as they create their "chair." Or, you may have to help with suggestions every step of the way. The process as much as the finished product is valuable for the observing students to see.

3. If you (or the class) are assisting the group in their task, you may help analyze what the different parts of the chair are:

   the back

   the seat

   four legs

   possibly two arms

4. If no one has volunteered, ask someone in the group to be the back. The person who is the back of the chair might stand tall and erect.

5. Next ask someone to be the seat. This person might crouch or kneel in front of the "back" with arms outstretched.

6. The four legs would go into position next, as would two optional arms.

7. When the process is complete, the class can clap to show their appreciation and it can be another group's turn.

Higher functioning students may not need much help. As they do this activity, they are imaging and working together on a nonverbal level and using many of the elemental skills of creative and improvisatory theater.

Variations

1. Give each group a secret assignment and let them work "independently" (with assistance if available) to create an object. At the end of the allotted time, groups can come back and recreate their object for the rest of the class, who will then try to guess what it is. Although the process is not observable, students are working cooperatively and independently toward a common goal. The end result can be appreciated.

2. Another variation can combine the study of another subject matter within the context of the game. For example, if you are studying the structure of a tree in science and what function each part of the tree performs, this activity could be extended in a different way:

   Give the assignment to a group of students to create a tree.

   Since the tree is a living thing, tell students that they may add some movement.

   The tree will have roots, a trunk, branches, and leaves.

   After the tree is created, take the time to let the class observe and appreciate the living "tree."

   You would then assume the role of an M.C. on an imaginary show called "Talking to Trees."

Holding an imaginary microphone, you "interview" the tree and its various parts. For example:

M.C.: "Here we are today on "Talking to Trees," and we have a beautiful—what kind of tree did you say you were?"

Trunk: "An oak."

M.C.: "Ah, an oak tree. Oak trees are good strong trees. And what have we here? (looking at the roots and holding out the microphone to the roots).

Roots: "I'm the roots."

M.C.: "Oh, and what do you do for the tree, roots?"

Roots: "I'm buried deep in the ground and suck up water and food to feed the tree."

This improvised kind of play dialogue, if started spontaneously, will often elicit spontaneous responses from the students, who will probably project themselves totally into the role they are playing. By "interviewing" each part of the tree, you can review what was learned in a science lesson in a way that is creative and activates a multitude of verbal and physical skills, as well as the imagination of all the participants.

Think about the areas you and your students are studying besides science, such as history or the community. What other objects could students create that would lend themselves to the dual purpose of learning and reviewing factual information?

Object Transformation

All theater games encourage working collaboratively and imaginatively toward a common goal.

Another vital aspect of working in creative drama is the use of objects to activate the imagination and facilitate the transformation of a character or circumstance. A prop is an object used in a story or play. The game of prop transformation takes an object out of the context of a story or play and isolates it to address the single challenge of using the imagination to change that object into whatever one wants it to be.

Activity Process

Estimated Time: One session

Suggested Music: Once this game is understood and flowing smoothly, you may play music softly in the background as students transform their props. Any slow to moderate tempo music would work.

Again, the observers play a vital part. When students transform their props, they will not say what they are doing. It is up to the observers (the rest of the class) to guess how the objects are being changed.

Transformation of props also implies transformation of characters, circumstances, and actions. The same skills of cognition and imagination used in the isolated challenges of this game can be transferred to drama activities such as plays or acting out stories.

You can organize this activity with a small group in front of the audience or with the entire class at once. The description here is for a small group "performing" in front of the "audience."

Level

Students must have the cognitive and imaginative abilities to be able to see an object, for example a rope, and then *understand* that it is a rope. Then, in their imagination, they can use that rope in a way that is fanciful and expands its function in the flexible framework of creative drama.

Benefits

- Cognitive skills
- Imagination and creative thought processes
- Ability to interpret abstract representations of objects and their function

Directions

1. Pick four to six students or volunteers. Have them stand in a line next to each, other facing the audience.

2. Take an object, such as a scarf, and explain to the students that they are to make this scarf into anything they can imagine. Without speaking but with physical gestures, they are to use the scarf as an object such as a towel, bridal veil, river, guitar, apron, or baby.

3. Each student in the line takes a turn. When the first student has "transformed" the scarf and shown it to the audience, the scarf should be passed to the next person in line, who should use the scarf as a different object, and so on until everyone in line has had a chance.

4. When the prop has made its way through the entire line of students, another prop and another group of students may be chosen.

    Following are some obvious ways in which something like a scarf might be transformed:

    Shawl (holding it around the shoulders)

    Bath towel (drying off after a shower)

    Handkerchief (blowing nose or waving good-bye)

    Dust cloth (cleaning gestures)

    Picnic table cloth (spreading on ground, laying out food)

    Blanket (lying down and covering up)

    Bullfighter's cape (holding it as though bullfighting)

    Following are some less obvious ways a scarf might be transformed. In the previous examples, the scarf, even though changed by function, still retained the quality of a piece of cloth. In the following possibilities, the imagination stretches even more.

    Barbell (With the scarf stretched lengthwise, hold it with both hands and use it like a barbell in weight-lifting. The scarf should be lifted as though it were very heavy.)

    Small puddle of water (The scarf is placed on the floor and the player dips his or her foot in it or splashes around as if it were water.)

    TV screen (Have two students hold up the square scarf. The player sits in front of it and watches, turning dials as if it were a television.)

    Basketball (The player balls up the scarf, pretends to bounce it, and "throws" it as though aiming for a basket.)

Adaptations for Higher Functioning Students

One thing that adds excitement to the process is to highlight the game aspect of the activity. This is more appropriate with higher functioning students who are working well with the idea of prop transformation. Have someone with a stop watch say, "Go," and within one minute (or whatever time you decide) see how many different transformations the group can make. When the prop has traveled to the end of the line of players, quickly start over again until time is up. Then do the same with a different group and the same or a different prop. The addition of the time element motivates quick thinking while breaking down inhibitions and hesitations, thus creating more spontaneity in the players.

Adaptations for Lower Functioning Students

Younger students and those who may not be able to grasp independently the idea of transforming a prop can still experience using their imagination in this way if you work closely with them. Choose a small group and sit with them in a circle. You can work with one scarf or supply everyone with one. You may have to initiate an idea and model it first. After the children understand that the cloth is a scarf, you may then show them a transformation. You may want to pretend you are using it as a towel, drying off after a shower. Ask students if they can tell what you are doing. If they can, hold up the scarf and say, "And so, what are we pretending this is?" If they have identified that you were drying off, they should be able to tell you that the scarf is being used as a towel.

Even if students cannot initiate an object transformation, have them perceive what you are doing and then give them the opportunity to do it themselves. By participating in this process, their imagination and cognitive abilities are being exercised. Acting out the use of the transformed object motivates the development of bodily kinesthetic intelligence and exercises the imagination. Answering your questions encourages speaking and the use of language.

Other Objects to Use for Prop Transformation Activities

- Piece of rope
- Yardstick
- Large sheet of paper
- Cardboard box
- Small can
- Large trash can
- Two candles or two rulers (see below)

These are objects easily found in or around the classroom. Following are some examples of how a pair of objects, quite different in quality than a scarf, might be transformed. The two objects could be two 12-inch candles or two rulers:

- Drumsticks (act out playing the drum)
- Rabbit ears (hop around like a rabbit)
- Handlebars of a bicycle or motorcycle (act out riding and holding onto the handles)
- Milking a cow (grip each object as an udder, making milking motions)
- Horns of a bull (paw the ground as if ready to charge)
- Conducting an orchestra (conduct using one or two batons)
- Steering wheel and stick shift (act out driving a car with one hand on the steering wheel and one on the stick shift)
- Reins of a horse (pretend to be riding a horse)
- Rungs of a ladder (pretend to be climbing a ladder)

It is a good idea for you to think through some of these prop transformations yourself, especially if your students are at a level where they will need some help getting started.

Progression of Object Transformation: Partner Improvisations

After your students understand the process, you may divide capable students into pairs, giving each pair a prop and telling them to work together alone for a few minutes and make up a scene between the two of them that uses the prop. After they have rehearsed (what is essentially an improvisation) they can perform their prop transformation scene for the class.

Although this can certainly be done in groups of more than two, having only two people keeps things very clear and simple. In the prop transformation scene that they create through spontaneous improvisation, the players have to share the same imaginative reality. If the scarf is a tablecloth for one player, the other cannot go wading in it as if it were water!

In this phase of the activity progression, the imagined scenario is taken one step further into the realm of creative drama where the fantasy becomes a "reality" to more than just one player. It is the beginning of dramatic interaction.

Developing Life Skills Through Drama

One of the greatest hopes and concerns that special education teachers have for their students is that they be able to function in society. Depending on the severity of a child's impairment, even the simplest daily task can be a major challenge. Being able to count out the correct bus fare, knowing where the bus stop is and where to get off, or even buying food at a store are basic skills that will help these children both now and later when they must get along independently as adults. Following is a list of some simple life skills many of these children should know, especially those who have the ability to live uninstitutionalized in society. Some are relatively frivolous and others are more necessary for day to day living.

- Buying a ticket for a movie
- Buying food from a vendor
- Purchasing specific items at a store
- Knowing how to use public transportation
- Applying for a job
- Dealing with a problem or conflict in various circumstances
- Making a simple meal

Make up your own list of basic life skills that you think are, or will be, important to your students, depending on what their abilities are:

1. _____
2. _____
3. _____
4. _____
5. _____
6. _____
7. _____

"Going to the Movies"

Activity Process

Estimated Time: Two or more sessions, at least one for preparation and warm-up and one for acting out the scenario. The number of sessions could be greater, depending on how many times you repeat a scenario with different students or how many different scenarios you do.

Suggested Music: No music

Level

Low to higher functioning. These activities, which can build life skills, are particularly good for lower functioning students who may in the future have difficulties functioning independently in the world. Because of the flexibility of the art form and the adaptability of the scenarios, you can tailor the goals of whatever life skill you are exploring to suit your students' needs and abilities.

Benefits

- Ability to perform practical tasks and recreational activities in society
- Ability to function more independently
- Development of confidence and self-esteem
- Interaction with others
- Understanding of processes necessary for accomplishing a goal in the world
- Verbal communication skills

Setting Up the Scenario

In these activities that can help special needs students develop and practice basic life skills, you will need to create a scenario and structure. Following are the three basic cornerstones of any dramatic situation:

- **WHO** (are the characters involved?)
- **WHERE** (is everything taking place?)
- **WHAT** (is happening and why?)

For this activity, the first thing you and the students must decide is what "make-believe" situation they would like to act out. One of the most useful skills for older and higher functioning students between the ages of 15 and 21 is applying for a job. However, for younger and lower functioning students, a simpler scenario might be something like buying a ticket for a movie or buying food from a street vendor.

Using the scenario "Going to the Movies," the **WHO**, **WHERE**, and **WHAT** can be fleshed out in more detail. (You may want to follow this format but substitute one of your own scenarios.)

WHO: Who is the main character? (the student)

Will there be anyone attending the movie with that student? (friend, parent, no one)

What other characters will be involved in the process of going to the movies? (people standing in line, person selling tickets, person collecting tickets, person ushering people to seats [optional])

WHERE: Where will the action begin to take place? (outside a movie theater)

WILL: you change from one location to another? (from standing in line outside the theater to going inside and sitting down)

WHAT: What is it that is happening? Why is it happening? What is the goal? (Here is where the sequence of events can be outlined.)

> Arriving at the theater
>
> Standing in line
>
> Buying a ticket from the ticker seller
>
> Going inside and giving the ticket to the person who collects the tickets and getting your stub back
>
> Going into the darkened theater and trying to find a seat with (or without) an usher's help

Go over the **WHO**, **WHERE**, and **WHAT** with your students until they are thoroughly familiar with the scenario.

Warm-Ups

1. Warm-ups and preparations for life skills drama activities can be the explorations that attempt to answer the **WHO**, **WHERE**, and **WHAT** questions.

2. Students may draw pictures of the scene outside the movie theater, with people standing in line. They could draw characters such as the ticket seller in the booth. They can draw the act of buying the ticket or giving the ticket to the ticket taker. Others might draw an audience watching the movie screen. These pictures are responses to what the students see inside their minds when you describe a character, an action, or a location. If you assign students different parts of the scenario to draw, or if they just happen to draw different parts of the scene, you might divide the pictures into like groups and put them in sequence on the wall, beginning with standing in line and ending with the audience in front of the screen.

3. Another warm-up would be a discussion of details of the physical surroundings of each location. Students can begin to find and gather props. The ticket booth could be a desk turned on its side. The ticket taker's location would have to be determined. Chairs could be set up in rows for the audience. A sheet or cloth could be hung as the movie screen.

Choosing Students to Be Characters

As always, a good way to start is by asking students what parts they would like to play. In this instance there would be

- The main student in line,
- Any friends who "came along,"
- Other people standing in line,
- The ticket seller,
- The ticket taker, and
- Other audience members in the movie theater.

Drama activities are very flexible. This particular scenario has many possibilities. If too many students want to be the main student in line, some can be the friends or family who are also attending the movie and would essentially go through the same process. Children who want to participate but have less to say or do because of lack of desire or ability can stand in the line and others can sit in the audience. If more than one student wants to be the ticket seller, you can have two or even three students pretend to help sell the tickets at several booths.

One way of limiting the number of students actively participating at one time but still give everyone a chance is to repeat the scenario, each time rotating different students into the roles of their choice. If yet more students are clamoring for active participation, the flexibility of dramatic activities such as these also allows for the creation of new roles. You might ask a particularly disappointed student what other role he or she could think of in this scenario. The student might say, "The person who sells popcorn!"—and a whole new part will have been created.

You must walk a thin line between letting enthusiastic students be involved or waiting their turn so as not to "overload" a scene with too many characters and detract from the objectives of the activity.

Beginning the Process of Improvisation

Improvisation in drama means acting that is spontaneous and not attached to a written script. Dialogue is not written down or memorized, nor are the movements or gestures of the actors.

Once you have had your discussion and drawing warm-ups, you may want to do another activity that extracts small bits and pieces from what might occur when the entire scene is acted out. You could ask for volunteers to show how they might perform one simple act taken out of context. Individual participation is thus increased so that students will not feel left out. It also helps students get ideas for their own improvisations in the scene.

Some of these "scenario snippets" are listed below. You can ask for volunteers to show the class how they would act them out. This can be done with or without words, or you may try it once silently and the second time with words.

- Show us how you would wait in line.
- Show us how you would buy a ticket for a movie. (The student must be able to take out money and hand it to the ticket seller. The seller could be another student or could be imaginary.)
- Show us how you would give your ticket to the ticket taker.
- Show us how you would buy popcorn.
- Show us how you would find your seat.

This warm-up will help clarify the different parts of the process when they are later acted out in sequence. It will also serve as a model for imitation and variation by other students.

Use of Conflict

Remind students about the most basic structure of any story, play, or even short scenario. There is a beginning, where things start, followed by a middle, which takes events through a process that leads to the end. In this case, the end is sitting in the audience watching the movie. The mission is accomplished.

In the true art form of drama, the middle of a scenario is usually where a conflict develops, and the end is when that conflict has been resolved. You and your students certainly have the creative option of introducing an imaginary problem or conflict somewhere between standing in line and watching the movie. Whether you do this will depend on how easy or difficult the basic scenario is for your students. If it is too simplistic, an imaginary problem like losing the movie money could make for an interesting improvised diversion from the original sequence of events. These problems are real possibilities and it is definitely worthwhile to explore how they should be dealt with. There are also the added creative options to decide on. Does the student finally find the money, and if so, where? (In a different pocket, on the ground, someone finds and returns it, etc.)

These occurrences can be fertile soil for bringing stronger emotions into a relatively run-of-the-mill scenario. Creative choices for an ending are expanded also. If the money is not found, does the student just go home, borrow money from a friend, or sneak into the theater? Appropriate and inappropriate behavior in a given situation can also be explored with the addition of conflict.

Children who are functional but emotionally out of control are likely to benefit from exploring conflicts and resolutions of those conflicts. Autistic and retarded students may be mightily challenged by the simple sequence of events that finally leads to being able to see the movie.

Directing the Activity

After all the decisions have been made and the warm-ups completed, you are free to try the scenario with one cast of characters. Adult aides can help keep children in their proper places in line or in the already occupied seats of the theater. In one of the first run-throughs, you may want to take a role such as that of the ticket seller so that by asking, "How many, please?" you can prompt a response from the first person in line. After that person answers, you can say, "That will be five dollars"—another cue that the students are to give you money.

You can change roles with each run-through or stay outside the acting entirely. Always feel free to coach your students to help them stay focused in that reality and to remind them what to do if they get lost in the process.

As you repeat the scenario, change character roles and scenarios and encourage the use of more talking. As students become more and more comfortable both acting and watching their classmates, their own perception of themselves will be clearer and they will become more confident in what they say and do.

Expanding on the Activity

In addition to adding conflict to the sequence of events, you may want to explore other details of the scene, such as the following:

- When is this taking place, day or night?
- What is the weather like? Is it raining or sunny? Hot or cold? How would standing in the rain affect the behavior of the people in line? What about prop ideas if it were raining? If it started raining, and only one person had an umbrella,, what might happen?
- If it is impractical to do so as a class, encourage the students to attend a real movie and, even if they are with their parents, buy their own tickets.

Audience

Every scenario that is improvised in this activity should be given positive reinforcement at its end. In addition to your comments of appreciation, audience appreciation is the best feedback any actor can get. Before the first round of acting, you might want to give the audience a few suggestions. Tell the students:

- Pay attention to what is going on. Watch the actors to see what they do. Listen to what they say.
- It is okay to enjoy the performance, but try not to speak while it is happening because that might distract the actors and keep others from hearing.

- If someone has something to say during the scenario, there will be a chance to talk about everyone's ideas when it is over.

- Laughing *at* someone is not a kind thing to do, but if something is supposed to be funny, it is okay to laugh.

- After the scene is over, show your appreciation by clapping. Booing is not permitted and could cause the "boo-er" to lose his or her turn as an actor.

This approach to learning life skills can be fun and have the bonus benefit of strengthening confidence and self-esteem. The scenes that you and your students create and bring to life through improvisation can be used as parts of longer plays or stories that may be created later in the year.

"Happy Legs": Emotions and the Body

In drama, an actor must develop his or her entire body as a vehicle for expression. The actor's senses and feelings must bypass the logic of the intellect and be experienced in every fiber of the actor's body. Although no one can literally "see" with their feet or "smell" with their elbows, there are imagination-based sensory and emotional body exercises that help train and strengthen the whole vehicle of the actor's being toward the end of more powerful communication and expression.

For special needs students, a simple transposition of this idea into the two realms of emotion and body will accomplish several things. On an artistic and human level, students will experience much of what actors do as they learn to function as an integrated person. Students will also learn about expressing emotion in a nonverbal way through the body, an isolated part at a time. Eventually the entire body can experience and express the emotion, but by isolating different parts to communicate and express feelings, there is a new perspective of being "in" the body. Finally, all this can take place through a process that is both nonthreatening and fun.

Activity Process

Estimated Time: One session

Suggested Music: Optional

Level

This activity is excellent for lower functioning students, but higher functioning students can have fun with it and derive benefits as well. Students should be able to understand the four basic emotions: happiness, sadness, fear, and anger. They should understand the emotions well enough to be able to focus a specific emotion in a particular part of their bodies. Some students may not understand this concept at first, but once it is modeled, they generally catch on fairly quickly. The flexibility of this activity allows you to work with whatever body parts children can move enough to express an emotion through them. Also, you may work with those emotions that your students understand and are most capable of handling.

Benefits

- Bodily kinesthetic sensations and movements associated with specific emotions
- Familiarity with isolated body parts
- Familiarity with four basic emotions
- Communicating nonverbally through the body and emotions
- Imagination in creating ways of expressing feelings through parts of the body

- Reading and speaking ability in the naming and recognition of written body parts and emotions

Preparation and Warm-Up

As a simple preparation, you might review the emotions: happiness, sadness, fear, and anger. A question such as "How do you feel when you feel happy?" really has no specific answer. However, if you ask a question such as, "How would you feel if school was canceled and instead you could go on a trip to the zoo?" and a student answered "happy," that student would be answering from the perspective of an imaginary experience. The understanding is emotionally experienced, stimulated by the idea of an imaginary situation.

You can also do a physical warm-up, a modification of the isolated body parts warm-up in the dance section. Bring the students through a series of movements with each part of the body, one at a time. No emotion should yet be attached to the body parts warm-up. If you are moving the head, it can move up and down or side to side. Fingers can move fast or slow. These directional and speed-oriented warm-ups bring students through a range of movement possibilities that they can refer back to when asked to put an emotion and body part together for nonverbal expression.

Directions

Children have fun with this simple activity. There is no distinct right or wrong. Only you can determine whether a child understands what he or she has been asked to do, since everyone's response to the challenge will be different.

1. Have students sit in a circle where they can see one another.

2. Ask a student to name any body part. A student might raise a hand and say "leg" or "legs."

3. Ask another student to name one of the four basic emotions you discussed in your warm-up. Remind them what those are if students have forgotten.

4. Pick a student or ask for a volunteer. Explain that, sitting in place or standing in the center of the circle, the student is to communicate a happy feeling, using only his or her legs. The result can be entertaining and some students will probably laugh.

5. After this student has shown one version of the emotion, you may choose another to show a different version. Go around the circle one at a time or have everyone do it together. Doing it together is probably best as a last step, since the process of observation of the first few individuals can be quite valuable to students in perceiving what is being communicated as well as clarifying what they are being asked to do.

6. To create choices that are more random, you might bring out two boxes. In one labeled "Body parts" you can put small slips of paper with one body part written on each piece, such as eyes, neck, head, toes, backside, or stomach. The other box, labeled "How You Feel," would contain the words *happy, sad, scared,* and *angry.*

7. Students could then pick one word from each box. If "fingers" and "anger" were picked, the students would show "angry fingers."

Variation

Estimated Time: One session

Suggested Music: Your choice

Materials

- Four index cards with one emotion written on each, folded in half, blank side out
- Four index cards with one body part written on each, folded in half, blank side out

Directions

There are many ways to put this activity into a game format that lets the combination of body parts and emotions occur by chance rather than by choice. This particular one promotes a creative collaboration between two students.

1. Have students form two circles. One circle will have the folded index cards with one of the four emotions inside. The other circle will have the index cards with the body parts written inside. The blank side is out.

2. Put on a piece of music.

3. While it is playing have students pass their cards around their respective circles.

4. At some point, stop the music and say "freeze."

5. Have the rest of the class form a large circle while the people left holding the emotion cards form a straight line facing the people left holding the body part cards, both lines in the center of the one large circle.

6. Pair up the students so that a student with an emotion is paired with a student with a body part.

7. Tell each pair to go to a separate corner (some may need adult supervision) and take only a few minutes or so—no more—to work out what they want to do to communicate their emotions through their body parts.

8. Combinations could be something like:

   sad neck

   happy elbows

   angry fingers

   scared shoulders

   Make sure each pair keeps their two words a secret.

9. Have each pair take turns performing their combination in the middle of the circle. The rest of the class must guess what emotion they are trying to convey through what body part.

10. If someone guesses correctly, everyone can be invited to do their own version of "angry fingers," or whatever it is, at the same time.

This activity can be extended and changed in many ways. Two body parts at a time can express emotions. Two people could express the same emotion at the same time, each with a different body part. With a little imagination, the possibilities are endless. Depending on where your students are cognitively and emotionally, other feelings or states of being such as shyness, nervousness, sleepiness, or boredom could be explored also.

Besides being fun and getting students in touch with their bodies and their emotions, the same skills of the imagination and the kinesthetic senses can be transferred and used in other creative drama activities.

Using Guided Imagery: Language Arts and More

Through your arts activities you have learned to function in many new roles such as choreographer, conductor, and drama coach. Using the process of guided imagery, you can lead your students to worlds inside themselves where they can explore with all their senses. With your voice and soothing words guiding them, students can focus on slowing their breathing and relaxing their bodies. Together, you can then travel to imaginary planets, mountaintops, underwater kingdoms, or tropical jungles.

Leading a group of special needs children in guided imagery is a skill that can be learned. Some teachers will automatically understand both the process and its value, whereas others will need instruction themselves. If you are able to be in touch with your imagination and speak in a stream of consciousness flow that stimulates the visual, tactile, olfactory, taste, and aural senses, you can create your own guided imagery exercises. If you would rather write your thoughts down first, you can read them to the class as they sit quietly with their eyes closed.

However, if you do not feel comfortable improvising or creating guided imagery exercises for your students, there is a wonderful book, *Spinning Inward: Using Guided Imagery with Children for Learning, Creativity, and Relaxation,* by Maureen Murdock (see "Drama Bibliography") . Even though this book is not specifically geared toward special needs students, it contains a wealth of information about guided imagery and how the senses are used in learning. It also contains accessible factual knowledge based on recent scientific studies about the function of the brain in the process of using imagery to learn. There are many examples of guided imagery that the author has created and used with her own students. These examples can be used with your students as well and be adapted to their level of ability.

What Is Guided Imagery?

Imaging is the process of "seeing" with your imagination. It is also the process of smelling, tasting, feeling, and hearing with the mind, stimulated by the images the mind creates. When imaging or imagery is "guided," someone is leading a person or a group through the process by gentle words and suggestions. Guided imagery, when effectively done, can be a powerful means of motivating and causing learning to occur.

Imagery is used in healing, relaxation, and stress reduction. Research has proven that learning is accomplished much more easily when the learner is relaxed and consequently more receptive. In a relaxed state, brain waves literally move more slowly and the wave patterns themselves are larger. Insulating ourselves from outside distractions, we can relax our bodies and minds to allow learning to occur in a very natural way.

Using the Whole Brain

The brain has been depicted as having two hemispheres, left and right. The corpus callosum is the system of nerve fibers that connect the two halves. When a person uses imagery in the process of experiencing and learning, information is sent back and forth from one hemisphere to the other. This actually facilitates the balanced development of both sides of the brain.

For any learning to occur, the entire brain is used, even though each side is responsible for specific functions. The left side of the brain processes information with logical, analytical, mathematical, and linguistic abilities, all of which are associated with the arts. The right side of the brain is responsible for the emotional, creative, intuitive, and other nonverbal thought processes and abilities in visual arts, music, drama, sports, dance, and aesthetic sensitivity.

Using imagery in your teaching will promote learning not only by helping to create a relaxed state of body and mind but also by allowing the brain to function holistically as images cross over from the right side to the left, where they are "translated" into logic or language.

Learning Through the Senses

Children begin life knowing and learning through all their senses. They think in images much more easily than adults. Yet as time passes, this natural inclination and ability will tend to decrease unless stimulated and reinforced in some way.

Studies at Stanford University have discovered that memory is stored in cells throughout the whole brain. Almost everyone has had the experience of having a particular odor or fragrance bring back a memory instantaneously, even if it was long ago. If senses are associated with learning (and much learning involves memory) it is called "cross-sensing." Children are very good at creating or accepting a suggested image and associating it with something that needs memorizing. For example, if a child is told, "Open up the big red door, and see that 3 + 1 is 4," they will probably remember it, based on the rhyme as well as the image. For some special needs students you can concretize that image externally by creating a big red door with the mathematical equation behind it. Later, the real red door can be removed and the image can remain. Language, math, and visual imagery have all synthesized to help something be learned. The image of the red door (from the right side of the brain) has crossed and connected to the logic, math, and language of the left side of the brain. The result is something strongly entrenched in the memory—and learned.

Using imagery in the classroom, guided, imaginary, or real and concretized, will help your special needs children to associate images or other imagined sensory experiences with things that need to be learned. For some, this will be a natural ability. For others, concretizing sense experiences with real objects and then removing them will help the ability to image with only the imagination. In all cases, the development of the entire brain is stimulated. Guided imagery is one approach to teaching and learning that is not used nearly so often as it should be in education. If you use books and resources, especially *Spinning Inward*, guided imagery can be a wonderful tool for you.

Poetry and Creative Writing Through Imagery

For one exercise in her book, Murdock recalls collecting a large variety of beautifully colored autumn leaves. She tells her students to sit comfortably, eyes closed, with legs crossed and palms up on the upper thigh. She then encourages them to focus on breathing deeply and slowly. Once everyone is feeling relaxed, she tells students to pretend they are sitting under a favorite tree as a gentle wind starts blowing. In between guided instructions, she allows a moment or so of silence so that the state of being and inner sensory and imaging can be experienced.

As she says that the leaves are falling, she gently drops leaves slowly and carefully over the children so they have the real physical sensation of feeling the leaves as they float down. She tells them to keep their eyes closed and pick up a single leaf. Holding it, they should feel the shape of the leaf, the surface, the edges, the veins. She asks them to touch the leaf to their faces and noses—to feel and smell it—to imagine the color. After some moments of this, children are encouraged to move their arms (and bodies) like gently falling leaves, and finally, slowly open their eyes.

The results of this exercise were beautiful poems in which tactile senses crossed with those of smell and sight. One child created a poem in which she wrote that the leaf "felt" red and tasted like "heaven." Even though this was not a learning exercise with a goal of logical knowledge, definite learning of a different kind occurred, as well as a stimulation of balanced brain development.

A creative writing exercise resulted from another guided imagery activity in which Murdock asked children to pretend they were their favorite animals. She took the children on a guided imagery journey during which they were to be those animals and experience everything she spoke about from the perspective of those animals: hearing, seeing, feeling, tasting, smelling, and functioning as those animals. Hands became paws, water was lapped up, and other animals were spoken to in the children's imagination. When asked to write about their experiences, very rich and colorful stories resulted.

These abilities, tapped by guided imagery, are some of the same used in creative drama activities. Students can act more convincingly if they are able to experience, inside themselves, a strong sensory or imagistic reality.

Taking the Initiative to Learn

The possibilities of guided imagery far exceed what is to be included in this handbook. *Spinning Inward* is full of ideas that will inspire you to make simple adaptations tailored to your own personality and abilities as well as those of your students. If you take the initiative, you will learn as much as your students.

Murdock includes instructions for creating an environment conducive to guided imagery and how to proceed step by step in a variety of different ways. The book also has guided imagery activities to enhance self-esteem, promote calmness and inner harmony, facilitate self-expression, improve verbal and nonverbal skills, and even increase cultural awareness.

Even though her book does not specifically address children with disabilities, it contains a wealth of ideas to enable you to speak the words that will guide your students on a magical journey. As much or more than any other approach to teaching, guided imagery contains the potential for many things that can enhance the quality of life, learning, and healing for the special needs student.

Storytelling and Storymaking

Storytelling as a Teaching Tool

From the beginning of time, long before the written word, there have been stories. The storytellers of many primal cultures were not just providers of entertainment but respected historians and teachers. In this role, it was their responsibility to pass on, from generation to generation, the traditions and knowledge vital to the survival of the society.

Stories have always been a way of educating young people in all aspects of life. Understanding and remembering a story is a natural result of listening to the storyteller weave all the colorful threads of knowledge into a narrative tapestry.

The languages of some Native American cultures do not include words for fairytale, folktale, myth, or legend. Loosely translated, a story told orally is called a teaching. With the voice and body, the storyteller brings the story to life with colorful words, strong emotions, sensory experiences, and visual imagery. Shared by the listener, these elements make storytelling one of the original and most powerful of teaching tools.

Motivation for Learning and Remembering

One of the surest ways to get students interested in any subject is through stories. Talking to students about American history will not involve them in the process of learning as much as having them write a story about some aspect of it. Even more dynamic is telling a story about a historical figure, such as General Grant, General Custer, or Sitting Bull. The Civil War, science, math, or any other curriculum area can come alive through stories.

Stories and Life Teachings

From the Grimm Brothers' tales to other cultures' myths and legends, story plots often revolve around conflicts that mirror those in a child's life. Problems with parents (*Hansel and Gretel*), doing what one is told (*Little Red Riding Hood*), or being loved and appreciated for what you are (*Cinderella*) are themes that any child would understand.

With these issues interwoven into stories, a child can identify with the plights and emotions of the characters. Good and evil as abstract concepts become concretized in a kindly prince or an evil queen. The negative results of bad actions or the positive results of good ones are also woven into the fabric of the story.

Even if these stories are unrelated to school curriculum, they contain teachings about life that illustrate a way of being in the world and interacting with other people.

Telling versus Reading

You may be hesitant at first to try storytelling without a book in hand. You may fear forgetting parts of the story or lack confidence about your ability to bring the story to life without the support of a written text.

When working with any student population, especially children with disabilities, storytelling, as opposed to reading a story, is a much more dynamic way to connect with their imagination. Free of the written text, you can establish more eye contact. By the adaptations you make in your preparation and the improvisations as you tell it, you are making the story your own and thereby making it more real for you and your students.

Preparing a Story for Telling

1. Choose a story with a plot your students will be able to follow. Aesop's *Fables* are good, as are stories like *The Three Little Pigs, Goldilocks and the Three Bears,* and *The Three Billy Goats Gruff.* These all use repetition in cycles of three. This cyclical repetition moves the story while also reviewing, in a less obvious way, what has just occurred. The sequence of events is also relatively easy to follow.

2. In preparation, read the story to yourself more than once. The first time, read it for your own personal enjoyment.

3. The second time, ask yourself:

    Where did I have the strongest emotional response?

    Where did I feel tension build up and release?

    What were the most powerful images or ideas that stayed with me?

    Being aware of your own responses and reaction to the story will influence many aspects of your telling: the pacing (how fast or slow you go in certain parts), how you portray your characters, when emotion will prompt you to use physical gestures or facial expressions, and so forth.

4. Make a list of the characters and how they relate to one another.

5. Outline the sequence of events. Note how one event relates causally to another. If you understand the chain of events, you will not be just memorizing; the plot will make sense to you.

6. Finalize any cuts, changes, adaptations, and clarifications.

7. Practice telling the story and tape yourself, if you wish. Tell it to the mirror—or a friend or a child. Note the listeners' reactions. Were you clear? When were they entranced? Bored? Ask them questions. When you tell the story, keep your own images of characters, places, and actions alive in your mind. This way you will be projecting the truth of your own inner experience.

8. When you can get through the entire story without forgetting major events and still keep your emotional connection to the material, you are ready.

9. If necessary, on an index card, make a skeletal outline of the plot and specific things you might want a character to say.

Fine Tuning Your Telling

Every time you tell the story, feel free to make changes and improvements. This is part of any creative process. Following are some things to think about as you become more and more comfortable:

1. Effective storytellers appeal to all their listeners' senses. The use of descriptive words that enhance visual, tactile, aural, and even olfactory and taste senses will enhance the emotional and kinesthetic experience of your audiences.

2. Use your face expressively. Make eye contact.

3. Think about the voices of the characters. Can you make your own sound effects at times? Where?

4. Physical gestures can be planned or improvised. "Canned" gestures, such as shrugging when in doubt or holding your hand over your brow when looking for something, are not as convincing or genuine as a gesture that grows out of a true emotion you are experiencing. In acting, the technique of "sense memory" is recalling a real situation in your own life in which you were sad or happy, angry, etc. By re-experiencing that feeling and transferring it to the story, facial expressions, voice quality, and physical gestures will be more real.

If the process of storytelling seems like a lot more work than reading a story, that's because in some ways it is. But the rewards and benefits for yourself and your students can be much greater also.

Storytelling by Individual Students

Having students tell stories individually, in front of the class, will promote the development of oral communication skills. Students with severe speech impairments, or who cannot speak at all, can listen to the teachers or other students tell stories or tell them using sign language. Depending on students' abilities, their participation in a storytelling unit can also include writing stories, drawing pictures of scenes from stories, acting out stories as others are telling them, or adding sound effects. For students who need to strengthen language skills, storytelling can provide a motivation for speaking, a structure to hold onto, and a guaranteed audience. Students who are severely limited in vocabulary and the ability to speak can attempt telling a story prompted by coaching and questions from you.

Polishing storytelling skills certainly need not be a primary goal for your students, unless of course a natural talent emerges. What is important is activating the imagination, translating feelings, images, and events into spoken language and communicating them to listeners. The teller must do this with all possible resources: the voice, the emotions, the face, and the body.

Level

Higher functioning students. To tell a story, a student should be able to speak and also be able to think about and understand a sequence of events, as well as the concepts of beginning, middle, and end. This can be an excellent activity for blind students. Deaf and nonspeaking students can tell stories through actions only or by using their own symbol system as you translate for the rest of the class.

Benefits

- Spoken language skills
- Cognitive thinking
- Imagination and visualization

• Communicating with emotion through the face and body as well as through language

Warm-Ups for Storytelling

1. If you are having students retell a familiar story in their own words, ask the class to help you recall the sequence of events. These can be put in a list or outline on the board.

2. Go over the main characters in the story and their relationships to one another. You can also list these on the board.

3. If you are having students tell a personal story, you might find a common theme such as:

    Getting up in the morning and going to school

    One of the happiest times in my life

    One of the saddest times in my life

    One of the funniest times in my life

4. Explain the concepts of narrator and narration, with or without the use of those words. Explain that a narrator speaks about what is happening in the story.

5. Let students know they may become a character and speak as a character if they like. You might take a few isolated instances and ask, "What did the wolf ask Little Red Riding Hood?" Have a student answer the question by being and speaking as the wolf.

6. If your students are able, have them write down a simple version of a familiar story, a true life story, or even an original story to help clarify it in their minds before attempting to tell it.

7. Have students draw pictures of images they see in their minds in the story. Have them show their pictures to the class and describe what is going on in each scene. This can be done before or after student storytelling.

Activity Process

Estimated Time: One session +, depending on how many students will be involved in storytelling

Suggested Music: No recorded music. However, other students may be able to help with sounds and sound effects to enhance a classmate's story. Later in the process, class instruments could be used.

The types of stories you can work with are

• Familiar stories,

• True life stories (see possible themes in warm-ups), and

• Original stories.

Directions

1. You might begin by telling your own version of a story. It might be easiest to choose one type of story for everyone. For example, if you and the class decide to tell a "true life" story with the theme "Getting up in the Morning," you could tell your version first.

2. Choose a student to tell his or her version of the story.

3. Remind the student that a story has a beginning, a middle, and an end, and that each story has characters, location, and objects. If necessary, help the child outline, verbally or on the board, the sequence of events in the story.

4. Allow the student to tell the story in his or her own way.

5. Positively reinforce the performance when the student is finished.

6. Ask the storyteller and the class what might be added (or changed) to make the telling of the story more real.

7. Keep in mind the following ways in which the telling of stories might be made more exciting. These include the use of

    Descriptive words (adjectives and adverbs) to add color and other emotional and sensory attributes to images and actions;

    Different facial expressions;

    Physical gestures; and

    The voice with expressive qualities, pacing (going faster or slower), or changing from the role of narrator to the role of a character in the story.

8. If the story is "Getting up in the Morning" you might ask:

    What is the beginning of your story? (getting up)

    What is the middle of your story? (getting ready for school, traveling to school)

    What is the end of your story? (arriving at school)

    What kind of day was it? (cloudy? sunny? rainy?)

    What color was the sky when you looked out the window? (blue? gray?)

    What sounds did you hear when you woke up? (birds singing, mother cooking breakfast)

    If your mother was cooking breakfast, what sounds did you hear from the kitchen? What foods did you smell cooking?

    When you washed your face, how did the water feel? (hot? cold?)

    How were you feeling? (energetic? tired?)

    Did anything special happen to make your story interesting?

    Were there any problems to solve? (a little brother or sister in the bathroom making you late for school?)

    What would make a good ending?

    These questions are only examples of one specific scenario, but they give you an idea of the kinds of questions you would ask to help students visualize and tell the story in a more powerful way.

9. After making decisions about the beginning, middle, and ending, and the use of descriptive words, you might explore more deeply some of the ways to make the story more real and exciting.

    Voice: The voice should be always used expressively. Also, the storyteller can become a character in addition to speaking as the narrator. For example, if the child says, "My mother told me to get up," you might ask, "How did she say it: happily, angrily?" Also, you can ask the child to tell it by saying something like, "My mother said, 'Get up, Jose!' " This way, the student will also speak as the mother.

Facial expression: When the mother's character speaks telling Jose to wake up, the face of the storyteller should reflect the emotion of the mother.

Physical gestures: When the mother speaks, the storyteller might put hands on hips or make a calling gesture with the hands around the mouth.

Sound effects: The storyteller can add sounds with his or her voice, mouth, or body. Other students can help out with class instruments or other sound sources. Wind blowing, birds singing, banging on a bathroom door, food cooking, and other events in the story might be enhanced by the use of sound effects.

10. Have the student retell the story. Afterwards, note and discuss the differences between the first and second telling. Also note any differences in the responses of the listeners.

Group Storytelling and Storymaking

The benefits of these activities are essentially the same as those of individual student storytelling. The students who participate might be less capable of telling an entire story but be able to contribute to a group effort in which the responsibility is shared. Consequently, there is the added benefit of developing the ability to work cooperatively toward a common goal.

Group Storytelling: Conducted Narration

For this activity, the entire class will be involved in telling the story. Each student tells a short segment of the story in sequence until a signal is given that it is the next student's turn. You "conduct" the story's narration by indicating with a nonverbal signal, such as a clap or a bell, that it is time for the student who is speaking to stop and for the next student to pick up the story line and continue.

The length of time a student speaks is up to you. Be sure to review the concept of narrator as a person telling the story and how to speak in the third person. If a student spontaneously becomes a character in the process of narrating, this is fine because it foreshadows the next activity of speaking only as characters in the story.

Activity Process

Estimated Time: One or more sessions.

Suggested Music: No music

Directions

1. Sit in a circle with your students.

2. Pick or have them help you pick a story that everyone is familiar with (*Cinderella, Little Red Riding Hood, Goldilocks,* etc.)

3. Review the sequence of events and characters before starting.

4. Ask if any students have questions about the basic story line or character relationships. If they do, help clarify any confusion.

5. You or a student begin to tell the story, in third person, narrative style. If a character emerges occasionally in the context of the narration, this is fine.

6. Signal with a clap or a bell when one student is to stop and another to pick up the story. Continue around the circle until the story is complete. (You may have to go around more than once.)

Group Storytelling: Speaking as Characters in the First Person

In this variation of group storytelling, students tell the story one after another around the circle as before, but this time they speak in the characters of their choice. This allows each student to experience the story from that character's perspective. They must choose an appropriate voice for their characters, understand what emotions the characters are feeling, and choose words to express what those characters will say in a way that will move the story line.

Higher functioning students might be able to jump in as characters, one after another, with only a signal from you to tell them when the "storyteller" character changes. Most likely, however, students will need some help. A simple phrase such as, "And so the Prince said . . ." will coach the student whose turn it is to speak. Students may be allowed to speak as long as you want them to, but they must always speak in the first person.

Before starting, review the story line again if necessary, as well as the characters and their relationships. Talk about voice types, personalities, and emotions.

Activity Process

Estimated Time: One or more sessions

Suggested Music: No music

Directions

1. Sit with your students in a circle.

2. Explain that this time you will be the only narrator. In this role, you will help them know when and possibly how to speak.

3. Tell them they should speak only in the first person, as one of the characters in the story.

4. If the story is *Cinderella,* it might begin as follows:

    Teacher/Narrator: "Once upon a time there was a girl named Cinderella. She lived with her stepmother and stepsisters who were jealous of Cinderella and made her work very hard."

    Here, you may indicate by pointing or a bell signal that the first student should speak. If the student is higher functioning, without any suggestion, he or she might jump in as the stepmother:

    Student 1 *(as stepmother):* "Clean the floor, Cinderella!" (bell signal)

    Student 2 *(as Cinderella):* "Okay, Stepmother. Oh, I'm so tired!" (bell signal)

5. If students do not grasp how to progress the story line from character to character without narration, you can jump in when necessary, saying something like "One day the stepmother said to Cinderella . . ." *(Student 1 speaks as the Stepmother).* You could then say, "And Cinderella answered . . ." *(Student 2 speaks as Cinderella).*

6. As you continue around the circle, your awareness of your students' abilities will determine when to step in and assist with your narration. As in all activities related in some way to drama, if you need to coach, cue, or speak out of your character as narrator, do so. Your role, in addition to propelling the story line, is to keep students on track and focused on the act of storytelling.

7. Continue this process until the story has come to its conclusion.

This version of group storytelling may, in some cases, produce rather disjointed results. However, the process of speaking in the first person and experiencing the perspective of a character both as storyteller and listener is more important than the smoothness of the story.

Group Storymaking

One way of creating original stories is by writing them. Storymaking is a simple but dynamic process of creating original stories as a group activity using spoken language. Stories are created from students' imaginations in a way that is spontaneous as well as fun. There will undoubtedly be some laughter as one student scrambles for ideas to complete the previous student's thoughts. Something that sets up expectations from the first part of a student's sentence could take an unexpected turn when the next student picks up the story.

Again, you will help establish the structure of the activity. You can act as "conductor" and use a bell or hand clap to signal when the story line is to be passed on to the next student. Because of the open-ended nature of a spontaneously created group story, you and the class may want to decide on a theme or title to help keep everyone focused. It could be as simple as "My Visit to the Zoo." This way, a setting and basic occurrence are given, around which students can fill in the details. Also, these kinds of stories can go on forever if left up to the students. To be able to bring the story to a close, you may want to establish, in the beginning, that a double hand clap or double bell signals that the story must come to an end with the next three students. As before, students may be narrators or characters, doing whatever comes naturally, unless you choose to limit them to one or the other.

Activity Process

Estimated Time: One session or more

Suggested Music: No music

Directions

1. Sit in a circle with your students.

2. Ask for a volunteer to begin the story, based on the agreed-upon title or theme. If there are no volunteers, you may start the story.

3. Students will contribute their part of the story one at a time around the circle. Let each student speak until he or she begins to lose ideas or until you sense it is a good time to change to the next student. Use the nonverbal signal to let each one know when to stop and let another start. An interesting time to change the storyteller is right before something crucial is about to occur. When the next student jumps in, what happens in the story is often unexpected.

4. Continue around the circle until you signal the story to end.

Once students catch on to the idea of group storymaking, they will probably want to do it again and again. Each time, the story can have a different theme or even the same theme, but events will be different. Repeating this storymaking activity gives students more opportunities to exercise their imagination. In the process, they will gain confidence and improve their verbal skills at expressing creative ideas. You might want to tape record or videotape the process so the children can see and hear what they created.

Story Theater: Acting Out Stories

Stories can be acted out by memorizing a written script or by improvising. Whereas written scripts must be carefully prepared by you or the students, improvisation is spontaneous, only requiring basic knowledge of the story line and agreement about who is portraying which character. The preceding activities of group storytelling and storymaking naturally lead to the next step of acting out stories in the form of a loosely structured play. This format is often referred to as story theater.

Making Choices

Story theater may or may not have a narrator, who tells what is going on and clarifies actions that are taking place between the characters' dialogues. You and your students may choose to act out the stories without a narrator. If this is the case, the students must know the story line well enough to move it, by themselves, through dialogue alone. Keep in mind that if you are the narrator, you can direct students from within the story. Your narration can keep them focused, let them know when to speak, and keep the story line on track.

The other important decision for you and your students to make is whether to improvise dialogue and narration or work with a script. Unless you are interested in play writing as a separate activity, which is rather advanced for younger or lower functioning students, remember that improvisation is fun and allows for creative spontaneity. It does not require nearly as much preparation as making a story into a play and memorizing the lines.

To summarize, your first two choices are whether to have a narrator and whether to improvise.

Improvised Acting Out of Stories

Most teachers and classes choose improvisation. If you choose this also, it is all the more important that there be clarity and structure to your approach.

1. Story line, sequences of events, places, characters, and actions should be agreed upon.

2. Who is playing which character must be decided.

3. You may want to divide the story into scenes. Three scenes can correspond to the story's beginning, middle, and end. It is also easier to remember shorter sequences of events in the context of one scene than an entire story.

Whether you are working with a familiar classic or an original story, narration combined with improvisation will facilitate a degree of focus and control while still allowing spontaneity and freedom of expression without the pressure of memorizing a script.

Props and Costumes

A simple object like a box can be transformed into a table by covering it with a scarf or colorful piece of cloth. Other objects in the classroom, with a little imagination, can also be used as props and enhance any setting.

Experimenting with simple costumes (scarves, hats, pieces of material as capes, etc.) can help children feel more like the characters they are portraying. Costumes help support the reality of the fantasy character, not only for the student who is acting but for the audience as well. Some of the handiest items both for prop transformation and costumes are large, colorful silk scarves. These can be bought from Indian or Pakistani stores for a reasonable price. They are washable, easily stored, and can vitally enhance any creative drama activity.

The acting out of stories may be casual or more performance-oriented. It is up to your own creativity how you would like to proceed. Just remember that your job is to organize the activity and keep the children focused on the "reality" of their fantasy for the duration of the story. Delegate responsibilities to your adult aides, if you have them. One can help with costumes, another can cue the entrances and exits of characters, and so forth.

Unless you are preparing for a school presentation on stage, the process of acting out stories can be limited to your own classroom. Students can take turns being the same characters, switching parts from scene to scene, or be in subsequent "performances."

As your students bring the story to life, an intimate group experience is bound to occur between the actors and their audience. You and your students will have just begun to taste the magic of theater.

Other Ways of Working with Stories

Because of the language demands of listening, telling, and speaking as characters, some lower functioning students may need more simplified approaches:

1. Ask questions to see what they remember of the events, including questions about how they pictured a character in their minds. What color hair did the princess have? How was she dressed?

2. One of the easiest ways for children to express what they visualized as they listened to the story is to have them draw a picture of it. They can draw scenes of places, characters, and actions that occurred. This kind of "looking back" (by reliving what was experienced and re-expressing it creatively through another medium) is a powerful way to reinforce learning. The children have to think about the experience and about what they thought. This process of higher order thinking deepens the learning experience.

3. If your students want to try acting but do not have the ability to sustain it through an entire story, work with one or two children, concentrating on one isolated scene. Help dress a child in a simple costume and assist him or her in speaking with another "actor." Far from being bored, the rest of the class will probably enjoy watching. If you have students take turns acting out simple parts of scenes, the experience of perceiving their classmates doing it first serves as a model.

4. If children have the cognitive ability to understand your words but cannot, for physical or other reasons, act out parts of the story, you might have them close their eyes while you relate a particularly descriptive segment of a scene. Ask the students to see "pictures behind their eyes" while you are describing what happens in the story. Tell them that later all of you will share what you saw in your imagination.

    Some children who can visualize may not have strong spoken language abilities. You can help them by asking questions to make them detail what they "saw," but in a way that requires only a word or two to answer. For example, if you are telling about an underwater journey, when you are finished you might ask, "What did you see?" With one word, the child could answer, "fish." Other questions along these lines, which require a minimum of words but specific visualization details, are:

    "Were the fish big or small?"
    "How many fish did you see?"
    "Were they different colors?"
    "What colors were the fish?"

    You can also go around the circle, one child at a time, and ask students to tell you what they saw.

5. A student must have the necessary physical and language abilities to write a story. Remember that writing an original story or rewriting an old favorite is a first step in one approach to writing a play. If students are writing stories, remind them to

    Be descriptive;

Use dialogue at times;

Focus on a problem or conflict, if there is one, and how to solve it; and

Remember the idea of beginning, middle, and end.

Stories have a multitude of possibilities that can be used to develop many of the intelligences. There is no one way to approach using stories. Your own creativity will determine how you decide to work.

Puppetry

In America, puppetry is generally considered to be appropriate for young children. In other countries, particularly those in the East and Far East such as India, Thailand, Burma, Japan, and Indonesia, puppetry has historically enjoyed esteem as a form of high art and has been respected by adult society. The traditions and moral values that the art of puppetry embodies in these cultures are as important as the myths and legends portrayed by the puppet dramas themselves.

Creating puppets and puppet plays with your special needs students can be a valuable and rewarding experience. All the elements of creative drama can be experienced through working with puppets. Young children will automatically become involved with the idea of puppets. Older children may view them as something only appropriate for younger children. Make sure you determine the attitudes that your children have toward puppets before beginning the process of working with them.

Puppet Plays

Puppets are motivating and stimulating for most children. For special needs children, they can be nonthreatening representations of people, animals, or even themselves. Because puppets are external and inanimate, special needs children are often less hesitant to express themselves verbally and emotionally to or through a puppet than they are to a human being.

Using puppets, particularly for performance, allows the student puppeteers to feel less nervous and even protected as they are hidden out of sight of the audience. Yet the process of rehearsing and moving the puppets at the right time, to recorded dialogue or to live speaking, activates auditory, linguistic, logical, visual, and spatial skills simultaneously.

Shy students can be transformed when out of sight of the audience and even become quite adept at projecting movement and emotion through their puppets. Manipulating the puppet in the context of a play or even a short scene challenges the student as puppeteer to make creative choices about how and when and why to move the puppets.

Considerations in Working with Puppets

When working with puppets, you are really working in two areas of the arts: visual art, in the creation of your puppet, and drama. Making the puppets will take several sessions, and creating and rehearsing the play will take as long or longer. Time considerations are important, as are the abilities of your students to sustain their interest and involvement in a project over an extended time period.

The type of puppets you can make will vary greatly and can be adapted to the motor skills of your students. Puppets made of toilet paper tubes on sticks or any other stick or rod puppet can simply be held in the hand. Puppets with mouths that move (such as the cereal box puppets described at the end of this section) require finer motor skills of the hands.

Deaf students may have trouble working with puppets since action is often primarily determined by aural cues and dialogue, taped or live. On the other hand, silent puppet interaction could be used improvisationally or to "act out" a familiar story.

Making Choices

When you decide to create a puppet play, there are several decisions to make. Do you want the dialogue audiotaped, written down, spoken live from a script, or improvised?

Experience has demonstrated that, for special needs students, manipulating a puppet and trying to read from a script at the same time is often unmanageable in live performance. Therefore, it is suggested that one of the following methods be used:

- Read from a script or improvise dialogue onto audiotape and have students move puppets in response to the taped dialogue at the time of performance.

- After adequate rehearsal, have students improvise dialogue live, with their own voices in the performance, as they manipulate the puppets.

- Have one student manipulate the puppet and another student speak for the puppet.

Dramatic skills will be experienced and developed in the rehearsal and taping process as well as in the performance. Your decisions, as usual, will be based on which approach is most suitable for your students.

Creating a Puppet Play

Activity Process

Estimated Time: Allow for as many sessions as necessary to create your play

Suggested Music: Optional; original or taped, appropriate to your play

Directions

1. Have the class choose a story with characters that will work with the puppets you have created, or, if the story is decided on first, you and the class may create puppets that will be the characters in the story. (See pages 76–77 for instructions for constructing puppets.)

2. Divide your story into scenes.

3. Make a list of the events in each scene. This will be the guide that helps students stay focused on where the action is going as things progress. Remember to keep things simple.

4. Pick characters for your puppets. Decide on costume additions to your puppets to make them more colorfully portray the characters they represent.

5. Decide which scenes will involve the most action. Find appropriate places for sound effects. Add dialogue.

Students can try acting out these ideas before writing them down or recording them. In doing so, the idea and characters become more concrete in the students' minds and they have a chance to see how their ideas work before using them with puppets.

Adaptations for Lower Functioning Students

If your students have trouble reading and writing, one of the most effective ways to create the voices and dialogue of characters for your puppet play is to have students improvise and record the dialogue on tape. Before the improvisation, review the sequence of events in each scene and let the children practice with each other what each character will say.

Keep the segments self-contained and as short as possible so that each can be rehearsed and recorded, one at a time. If a mistake occurs, simply rewind the tape and try again.

Improvisation and Taping for Higher Functioning Students

This technique of verbal improvisation onto tape is also appropriate for students who are capable of reading but haven't the patience or ability to write out a script. If you want to have them read from a script, their taped improvisations can be transcribed, perhaps by you, into writing. This can serve as the beginning of a written script, which can be touched up and rehearsed. If your students are able to write a script, make sure they have a sufficient amount of rehearsal before recording it.

Things to consider in the reading of the script, whether live or into a recorder, are

- The voice types of the characters;
- The timing of who speaks when and in what sequence;
- The pacing of how much time to allow between different events; and
- Where to add sound effects, silences, and taped or original music.

Creating Your Puppets

There are numerous ways to construct puppets. If you are going to make a play based on a traditional fairytale, students may want to draw pictures of the story's characters before creating their puppets. One of the best books on theater arts for special needs children is *Wings to Fly* by Sally Dorothy Bailey (see "Drama Bibliography"). She not only explores, in great depth, various ways of bringing creative drama experiences to children with special needs, but she also devotes an entire section to puppets and puppetry. Some of the puppets she describes are

- *Finger puppets:* Created to fit onto the tips of fingers. They require fine motor skills and are not always practical for live performance. Videotaping is a possibility.

- *Rod puppets:* These are puppets that are attached to a rod or stick. More complex rod puppets have sticks attached to the puppet's arms or hands to allow independent movement.

- *Simple hand puppets:* These are made out of any material from fabric to socks to paper bags or Styrofoam balls and are constructed in such a way as to fit over the hand of the puppeteer. The little finger and the thumb move the puppet's arms while the index and/or middle finger support the puppet's head.

Puppets can be constructed from wooden spoons (the spoon is the face); paper bags (simply drawing a face at the top of the closed end of the bag and inserting fingers into the bottom fold of the bag to make the mouth move); various sizes of cardboard tubes attached to sticks, with face and body drawn onto the tubes; and even from paper plates, simply glued onto a stick or folded in half (for talking puppets).

Cereal Box Sock Puppets

Following is a detailed description of how to create a puppet that will have a mouth that can be manipulated so it can "speak." The main materials are a sock and a small cereal box.

Materials

- Small (individual serving size) cereal boxes (gelatin boxes or other small, light boxes work also)
- Blunt-tipped scissors

- White glue and/or hot glue gun (the latter for teacher's use only)
- Socks (large enough to fit a hand into). **Note:** White socks allow for all kinds of possibilities, but if you know ahead of time what kind of animal your puppet will be, consider a black sock for a skunk, a green sock for a snake or frog, an orange sock for a tiger, and so forth.
- Fabric scraps, yarn, sequins, felt, feathers, pipe cleaners for facial features, or pieces of clothing like ties or hats.
- Tape
- Permanent colored magic markers or Sharpie felt-tipped pens.
- Optional: Store-bought plastic eyes, buttons, or beads.

Activity Process

Estimated Time: One to three sessions

Suggested Music: No music, unless softly played in the background as children work.

Directions

1. Tape closed the open end of the box.

2. Cut across the middle of one of the broad sides of the box and down the two narrow sides, leaving the other broad side uncut. Depending on your students' abilities, you may need to cut the boxes ahead of time.

3. The boxes then are folded in half in the middle of the uncut side. Show your students how to put their fingers in one half of the cut box and thumb in the other half. When they open and close their fingers and thumb, the puppet's mouth will work. You may want to reinforce the fold in the box (the back of the mouth) with tape to make it stronger.

4. Have the students cut off the toe of the sock approximately two to three inches from the toe, depending on the size of the sock. Again, you may wish to do this in advance.

5. The box is then folded in half along the fold so that the two openings (where you put your fingers and thumb) are open, side by side.

6. The open toe of the sock is slipped over the open end of the folded box. If the toe opening is too small, cut off a little more.

7. Using white glue or the hot glue gun (teacher operated), glue the sock to the box.

8. Depending on what kind of glue you used and how fast it dries, you may either proceed or leave the following steps for another session.

9. Have your students paint or glue fabric scraps or felt on the cardboard nose (beak or muzzle) of the puppet, covering it completely. They may also glue fabric or felt to the mouth area in the appropriate color, adding tongue and teeth if desired. (Children must work carefully since the glue takes a moment to set.) Another alternative is to paint the inside of the mouth and add a felt tongue. These are creative decisions that you and your students will make based on their abilities, your materials, and time constraints.

10. Add ears, eyes, and other details. Eyes can be made from black and white felt (or yellow and green felt if the puppet is a snake), or pre-made plastic eyes can be glued on.

11. When the puppet is dry, students may slip their hands up through the sock and try activating the mouth, bringing the puppet "to life."

12. Other additions to give puppets more character would be manes, collars, ties, or hats. If you are using your puppets to act out a favorite story, the class could actually fashion "costumes" for your puppet characters. (A puppet can become Little Red Riding Hood with something as simple as a red scarf tied around its head; the grandmother could wear a "shawl" and a pair of pipe cleaner glasses.)

Making a Puppet Stage

You can use bookcases or rectangular tables turned on their sides and covered with black or other solid color material to use as a puppet stage. More elaborate stages can be constructed by aides, parents, or older students with metal or wood frames and hanging material on the frame in an appropriate way. The important considerations about your stage are

- That it be sturdy and not collapse,
- That there is sufficient room behind it for the puppeteers to be comfortable, and
- That it successfully conceals the puppeteers from the audience.

There is no set formula for creating your puppet stage. You will probably make your creative decisions based on materials, help, and time available. For puppet plays involving only two or three characters, a large cardboard box could have a section cut out of it and two or three children could kneel inside. For stages that will accommodate wheelchair-bound students, a large piece of black material suspended across part of the room will allow easy access in and out for the chairs. Fabric can be pinned or attached with Velcro to bookcases, closets, or walls, or it can be hung sheet-like on a suspended rope, then detached or pulled back as children are wheeled behind it.

Closure and Follow Up

Videotaping your puppet performance is a wonderful way of letting the puppeteers view what they have accomplished. It is also a way for both you and your students to reflect on and re-appreciate the fruits of your journey—from creating your puppets to making them come alive in a final performance.

Drama Glossary

Act. To cause something to happen.

Action. The occurrences between two actors or parts of a drama in which something is happening physically, emotionally, or otherwise

Actor. One who acts or takes on the role of a specific character in a play or drama activity.

Audience. Those persons perceiving the dramatic action on stage. An integral part of the creative experience of theater.

Character. A real person or the physical expression of that person.

Coaching. Assistance given to student actors by teachers working in the capacity of director. Coaching is to help keep the actors focused and prompt them should they have memory lapses.

Conflict. A struggle arising from opposing needs.

Creative drama. An improvised and informal dramatic event that may be the acting out of a short scenario, scene, story, or fairytale.

Dialogue. Words spoken or conversation between two or more actors in a play.

Director. One who acts in the capacity of helping actors decide how to say their lines; when, where, and how to move on stage; and, in general, to make creative contributions to whatever dramatic activity they are involved with.

Imaging. Creating a picture or an image in one's mind.

Improvisation. Making spontaneous decisions about what to do in a dramatic context. Interacting and communicating with others spontaneously.

Mirror. To reflect back, physically or emotionally, the actions or feelings of another person.

Monologue. Words spoken by a single actor, although not necessarily to another actor. The monologue expresses inner thoughts and feelings, with the audience as the listener.

Playwright. A person who writes scripts for plays.

Prop. An object used on stage during a play or dramatic scene; helps strengthen the reality of the drama.

Radio play. A play that is recorded from a written or improvised script that features the voice only.

Role-playing. Taking on the characteristics of a specific person.

Set. The scenery, furniture, props, etc., used to create the illusion of a specific environment in a play or dramatic scene.

Story theater. A theater format in which stories are acted out, with or without narration. Stories can be traditional, classic, or original.

"Who, what, where." The three main cornerstones that help define any dramatic situation. Who refers to character and character relationships; what refers to what action; where refers to the location and setting.

Drama Bibliography

Bailey, Sally Dorothy. *Wings to Fly: Bringing Theatre Arts to Students with Special Needs.* Rockville, Md.: Woodbine House, 1993.

Dayton, Tian. *The Drama Within: Psychodramas and Experiential Therapy.* Deerfield Beach, Fla.: Health Communications, 1994.

Murdock, Maureen. *Spinning Inward: Using Guided Imagery with Children for Learning, Creativity, and Relaxation.* Boston and London: Shambala, 1987.

Spolin, Viola. *Improvisation for the Theater.* Evanston, Ill.: Northwestern University Press, 1976.

———. *Theater Games for the Classroom: A Teacher's Handbook.* Evanston, Ill.: Northwestern University Press, 1986.

CHAPTER THREE

Music

Music gives soul to the universe, wings to the mind, flight to the imagination and life to everything.

—Plato

Music and the Power of Sound

The next time you are able to sit alone someplace where you can feel part of nature, listen to the whispering of wind through the trees, melodious birdsong, the buzzing click of cricket rhythms, and out of nowhere, the startling cry of a crow. You may hear hushed shimmering ripples from an invisible stream, continuous colorful patterns of sound rising to a frenzied crescendo and then dying to utter silence. Just listen.

Whether listening to a piece of music or sounds in nature, you are hearing the vibration of energy as it becomes audible in the physical world. A child can wave his or her arm through the air in silence, yet with that same gesture and energy, hold a stick and strike a drum, creating what we call *sound*.

Sound is energy and energy is sound, whether we hear it or not. Both are caused by vibrations. But when that energy comes in contact with physical matter, it becomes audible through the specialized organs of our hearing and, in subtle but powerful ways, audible to our entire bodies.

It is no wonder that children respond spontaneously to sound and music. We cannot see music as we can the creative products of visual arts, dance, or drama. But for the child with severe disabilities, even a single sound can be fascinating. Eastern philosophy holds that there is a universe of music in a single sound. Nowhere will you find more proof of this than in seeing a child who cannot speak or can barely move respond with amazement and wonder to the single tone of a bell or a flute being played softly and intimately into his or her ear.

The hypnotic pull of regular beats and the repetitive rhythms of sounds organized into patterns of music can lull us into the long-lost comfort and security of our mothers' wombs and the heartbeats that gave us life. Vibrations of sound through the air penetrate the energy fields around our bodies, bypassing language and logic, to move us, inexplicably, to the depths of our feelings where all human beings share an unconscious connection.

From the perspective of pure physics, all things on this physical plane are manifestations of different vibrational frequencies. Sound, traveling as pure, invisible vibration, can so powerfully affect our emotions, state of mind, and physical well-being that we are intensely moved without ever having been "touched."

Sound and music can be powerful allies in reaching students who have disabilities and transforming even fleeting moments into magic. Tap into the musician within you. Give your students the gift of sound.

Music and the Special Needs Student

Throughout time, learning to play or sing music and acquire the skills of deciphering a new language in sound and symbols usually have required one-on-one instruction. Even so, the ability to have a personally profound listening experience resides in us naturally whether we are trained or untrained; whether we listen to a single sound or an entire symphony.

For special needs students, working with sound and music in a most simple or a sophisticated way will stimulate almost all areas of the intelligences: bodily kinesthetic, visual and spatial, linguistic, logical mathematical, interpersonal, and intrapersonal, as well as others (creative, emotional, etc.).

In everyday life, our ears are usually processing and interpreting sounds for functional rather than aesthetic reasons. Hearing, creating, and interpreting sound develops aural skills that share the commonalities of skills demanded by spoken language: a sense of a sound occurring over time, the highness or lowness of a sound, the speed and rhythmic pattern of sound, the loudness or softness of sound and the importance of that crucial element, silence. How single sounds are connected and organized into musically meaningful phrases is analogous to how words and sentences are formed from the basic alphabet.

Creative self-expression through sound without the commitment to the meaning of the spoken word can release pent-up emotional, as well as physical, energy. In addition to intellectual development, working with music and sound can be calming or stimulating, depending on the nature of the activity. Participating in sound activities as either leader or follower also can increase a child's sense of self-worth, self-confidence, and accomplishment.

How to Begin Working with Music and Sound

You are not expected to have the expertise of a trained musician to use the activities in this section. They are designed to inspire what you can do, not what you can't do. Following are some simple suggestions to ease yourself and your students into the world of sound and music:

1. Listen to music in your classroom. Offer your students a balanced musical "diet" from the many genres available. In addition to what they choose to hear, expose them to the beauty of great classical masterworks as well as the rhythms and artistry of jazz and music from all global cultures.

2. Go on a walk with your students and listen to the sounds of nature. Listen to the wind, birds, insects, and rushing water. Point out to them the sounds of cars or planes in the distance. Collect "sounds" and take them back with you. Recreate the sounds with mouths and bodies, or with rocks, sticks, and dry leaves you have collected. Make a " sound collage" of the woods or tell the story of your walk in pure sound.

3. Move to music. Let your children move their bodies and feel the rhythms, melodies, and colors of sound. Watch the music enter their ears and come out in expressive movement.

4. Begin a day with music; end a day with music—or do both.

Do what you can do and never ignore the obvious or seemingly simple. Sound is so powerful and evokes such a strong primal response that working with some of the listed ideas—adapting them to suit your students' comprehension and coordination—will give you days and weeks of ideas to enhance your teaching.

 # How Sound Changes in Music

Listening to sound for sound's sake, out of context of its everyday functions, can hone students' listening skills. As you work with music in your classroom, remember that there are ways that sound changes in music as well as in life.

Being able to hear, identify, produce, and interpret these sound changes can have a profound effect on students' abilities, not only to enjoy or create music, but also to hear, interpret, and express themselves through spoken language.

The Basic Ways Sounds Change

High	Low
Fast	Slow
Long	Short
Loud	Soft
Sound	Silence

Please note that high and low refers to the highness and lowness of pitch (such as the difference between a little girl's voice and that of a full grown man). Some students will confuse high and low with loud and soft. Also, when working with high and low, take care about the highness and lowness of instrument positions in physical space. For example, a low sounding instrument might be held higher in space when played than a higher sounding instrument. This could create confusion in a child who is visually focused on physical space instead of aurally focused on the sound being played.

 # What Makes Music?

Sounds can change, but that does not necessarily create "music." Composer Edgar Varèse defined music most concisely; "Music is organized sound." (With similar reasoning, dance could be called "organized movement.") This simple definition refers only to the organization of the elements of music such as pitch, rhythm, harmony, and timbre (see "Music Glossary" for definitions). It does not define what happens inside the listener when the resulting organized form of those musical elements transcends the sum of its parts to touch and move us in powerful and mysterious ways.

Working with your students in sound and sound organization (music) activities will aid development in all areas of their intelligence.

 # Form in Music

Form is the "sound shape" that occurs as a result of organizing musical ideas. It is a kind of blueprint of the structure of the music.

Music and dance both deal with the element of time. Dance involves physical bodies moving through time and space. Music is sound moving through time. Form in dance is the organization of movement ideas. If you have movement idea **A** (turn in a circle) and movement idea **B** (jump in the air), when you create **ABA** (turn in a circle, jump in the air, turn in a circle), you have the microcosm of dance form.

Because movement can be seen and felt, it is generally easier for most people to work with than sound, which is invisible and less rooted in physicality. Yet form in music comes from exactly the same principle as form in dance: the organization of ideas, but ideas created by sound.

A piece of music must have the following three things:

Sound(s)

Idea(s)

A plan

The sounds can be simple claps and stamps. The ideas could be **A** (clap three times), **B** (stamp twice). The plan could be **ABA** (clap three times, stamp twice, clap three times). As simple as this example is, it is a seed that can be expanded upon to create longer musical forms. New ideas **C** and **D** could be added to alternate with idea **A**, creating an **ABACADA** or "rondo" form.

Keeping in mind that music can be thought of as organized sound, you and your higher functioning students may certainly rise to the challenge of taking these ideas to the next level by making creative choices, organizing sound ideas, and creating your own music forms.

Sound Sources for Your Music Activities

The mini-activities associated with each category of "sound sources" are a way of further exploring each source and introducing a simple structure for the use of these sounds. In a very basic way, this will illuminate some of the elements involved in music making.

Finding sounds is fun. But it is important to give students some special applications as soon as possible so that it becomes evident to them that these sounds are going to be used in a way that is different from anything they normally experience.

The sounds you use may come from a variety of sources.

Classroom Percussion Instruments

If you are lucky enough to have percussion instruments at your school, they are a wonderful resource and can be integrated into experiences with other curriculum areas. Instruments can be used in dance and movement activities, to provide music and sound effects for drama and storytelling, or to illustrate certain principles of science or mathematics.

Class percussion instruments usually consist of small drums, xylophones, sticks, jingle bells, triangles, tambourines, and other such durable and easily played instruments. If you need to purchase these yourself, most music stores have student-level instruments. There are also music and other educational resource catalogs from which instruments can be ordered. More and more of these catalogs are offering student versions of ethnic folk instruments from South America, Africa, Asia, and elsewhere.

Found Sounds

Ask students, with their parents' consent, to bring materials or objects from home, such as egg beaters, strainers, pans, or pan lids. A nature walk can yield stones, sticks, or clusters of dry leaves on twigs, all of which are potential sound sources for music activities. A "sound hunt" can be undertaken in the classroom if handled in an orderly way. Pencils can be tapped on the bottom of empty cans. Rulers can be hit or slapped together. A trash can may be used (with restraint) as a drum. Containers of metal or plastic, with secure lids, can hold anything from pennies to paper clips, beans, or marbles. Closet doors may be thumped and desk tops tapped.

When exploring found sounds in the classroom, it is important to keep the process controlled so that it does not become a free-for-all. Following is an activity to add a gamelike dimension to your sound search.

Sound Scavenger Hunt

Divide your class into two or three teams, with adequate adult supervision. Each team is to find sounds and bring them back to show the class. The minimum should be one sound per person on the team. One team can search the classroom. One team may go outside to look. Another team might be allowed to search the school for sounds.

After the period of time allotted, all the teams should report back to the classroom with their sounds. Depending on the functioning level of the students, you may choose various ways to have them present their sounds to the rest of the class:

Option 1

- Have students demonstrate each found sound one at a time.
- Have students demonstrate all the found sounds together at the same time.
- Do both of the above.

Option 2

- Choose a leader (conductor), perhaps starting with you, the teacher, modeling the process.
- The conductor can point at any sound he or she would like to hear.
- The conductor may have one, two, three, or more sounds play together.

For more details on "conducting," starting, stopping, cueing, etc., see "The Conductor's Gestures," page 107.

Option 3

- Higher functioning students, as a class and with adult help, can choose a familiar story or make up a simple story and use the found sounds to "illustrate" the story with sound.

Any one of these options could be a full-blown activity were it to be explored in depth. Even if your students cannot create a real piece of music at this time, there will still be an element of creative thought and choice making in using sound. These simple challenges will set the stage for other sound and music activities you might lead later on.

Body Sounds

Hand claps, slaps to the thigh, and finger snapping are all examples of body sounds. With or without modeling an example of your own body sound, go around the room and see if each student can demonstrate one body sound. If all can do this, go around again and have them make two body sounds. You might even try for three.

If this is successful, have students explore the way sound changes by asking them in turn to "play" their body sounds in any of the following ways:

- Loud
- Soft
- Fast
- Slow
- Any of the above in combination

In music, sound also changes from long to short and high to low. Sound can also alternate with silence. However, for your purposes, body sounds are perhaps best suited to the sound changes suggested above.

Mouth Sounds

Although at first it may seem that mouth sounds might work for children who cannot speak, there may be a problem with making these sounds repeatedly, on cue, or in a rhythmic pattern. Clicking, clucking, croaking, and pulling air inward through tightly puckered lips are all examples of mouth sounds. Using the following consonants repetitively or in different rhythms is also a creative way to use mouth sounds:

- "Chh, Chh, Chh"

- "kkk, kkk, kkk"
- "tt, tt, tt"
- "sss, sss, sss"
- "ff, ff, ff"
- "p, p, p, p"
- "whh, whh, whh"

Think of others or ask your students to come up with new ideas. These mouth sounds do not use the vocal cords, but are produced by creating oral friction, using the tip or other parts of the tongue, lips, teeth, or cheeks with puffs of air.

Mouth Sound Improvisation

Have everyone try one sound together softly, such as "sss" or "chh." The sound should be soft, almost like a whisper.

Variation 1

- Lead the entire group in softly repeating the same sound, such as "Chh, Chh, Chh, Chh . . ." over and over in a steady beat.
- Have a volunteer or one student improvise a "mouth sound" solo over the mouth sounds of the group beat. This means that the improviser may also use "Chh" or make whatever mouth sound he or she chooses over the group beat. The soloist should try to be louder than the group and can use any combination of mouth sounds and rhythms in the solo.
- Repeat the process with other student soloists.

Variation 2

- Divide the class into two or three groups. The groups should be fairly small (two to four students in each).
- Have all groups but one keep a steady beat with the same mouth sound.
- Have one group at a time improvise mouth sounds together over the steady beat created by the rest of the class.
- After one group has improvised, have them join the steady mouth sound beat. For a moment, the entire class will be doing the beat together. (Try to keep the beat going at all times even as you change "solo" groups.)
- Choose the next group and signal them to begin their group solo improvisation.
- Continue the process until all groups have had their turn to improvise using mouth sounds.

Note: There may be a tendency for some students to try to make a joke of this and create "offensive" sounds with their tongue and lips. Going through the consonant possibilities and other sounds as a class, with you modeling when necessary, should help prevent this.

Vocal Sounds

Vocal sounds, which utilize the throat, vocal cords, larynx, mouth, and lips, are very valuable as exercises for children who have difficulty forming precise words but can vocalize basic sounds. Because vowels and the voice itself are used, these sounds may easily be made longer or shorter in duration, simply by drawing out or shortening the vowel sound. Following are a few examples:

Vowel Sounds	Consonant Sounds
AH	MMM
OO	NNN
OH	B(uh)
EE	D(uh)
AY	G(uh)
AW	L(ull)
EH	RRR

Sound Changes in Music with Vocal Sounds

1. Choose any one of the listed sounds.

2. Have the students make it together.

3. Leading the group, have them explore, individually or together, the following sound changes:

    loud—soft

    high—low

    fast—slow

    long—short

    sound—silence

4. Choose another sound and repeat the process.

Emotion and Sound: How Am I Feeling?

Wolves howl, pigeons coo, cats purr, dogs growl, and blue jays shriek. Sound as an expression of emotion has universal commonalities that go beyond culture and even beyond being human to the collective essence of all life. Loud, rough sounds can indicate anger or fear. Soft, slow, low sounds might signify sadness or contentment. Lighter, higher, and faster sounds could mean happiness.

1. For this simple sound exploration, write the four basic emotions (happiness, sadness, anger, fear) on pieces of paper and put them in a container. (If students cannot read, draw four simple circle faces with these expressions.)

2. Choose four volunteers and have each student pick one piece of paper from the container. If a student cannot read, the emotion can be whispered into his or her ear, or the pieces of paper can have the faces drawn on them with the written word. Students should keep their "emotions" or designated "feelings" secret and show no one.

3. Have the four students line up in front of the class with their backs to the class.

4. Using only the vocal sound, "AH," students should express the emotions they chose. No facial expression or body movement is allowed; only sound, and only on "AH."

5. Remind students that although they can only use the sound "AH," they may use any of the previously explored sound changes. (You may need to model these again to remind them.) The "AH" may be long, loud, and high; low, short, and soft; or any combination.

6. As each student takes a turn, have the rest of the class guess what emotion the vocalizing student is trying to express.

Note: You may post the words, drawn faces, or cut out pictures of people registering these emotions on the blackboard so students can match the emotion expressed to the words or pictures.

This kind of sound awareness in relation to emotion can later be translated into the playing of instruments (see "Mood Duets," page 101). It is also useful when using music to enhance drama or storytelling.

All of the sound exploration activities are excellent warm-ups for other music activities. Using the body, mouth, and voice as alternative sound sources provides a visceral experience with most elements of music, such as pitch, volume, rhythm, timbre, and emotional expressiveness, which can all later be transferred to an instrument.

Instrument Making

Making instruments will require substantial adult help and supervision even with higher functioning students. Depending on the students' comprehension, ability to follow directions, and physical coordination, you may choose to do one instrument per student, or one instrument per group of students (i.e., one table of students with instrument materials and one or two adults per table to create one instrument). In some cases, one instrument per class can be more of a "demonstration activity" if the students are higher in cognitive ability than physical coordination.

The process of instrument making develops fine motor coordination, spatial awareness, sound perception, and making creative choices related to the specific timbre (sound color) that students will want to hear. (Do they like the sound of dried beans being shaken in a plastic bottle, or the sound of uncooked rice? What about the sound of a metal container as compared with a cardboard box?)

Percussion instruments produce sound by being struck, tapped, scraped, rubbed, shaken, or in some cases, plucked. Instruments may be decorated as you choose. The important thing is that they make a sound. (See also "Making an Ocean Drum" in the Visual Arts chapter.)

Activity Process

Estimated Time: These instruments can take only one session, but they usually require more than one. How long they take dependents on how much preparation can be done ahead of time, the number of adult facilitators, and the level at which your students can function visually and physically.

Suggested Music: Any background music can make an instrument making activity more enjoyable. However, Central South American or African music that uses any of these instruments would be particularly suitable.

Level

Higher functioning students may work individually or in small groups with adult facilitators. Lower functioning students may be helped with hand-over-hand assistance or work as a class.

There are also instruments that are extremely simple to make for students with fewer physical or cognitive abilities.

Benefits

- Visual and spatial awareness
- Fine motor coordination (if students can work hands on)
- Sound awareness
- The ability to follow directions

Sistrum

A sistrum is a percussion instrument (also known as an *idiophone* in world instrument classifications) indigenous to Ethiopia and other African countries. It is essentially a stick with a "Y" shape, the tail being the part that is held. Many branches have this natural shape and can be used as the body of your sistrum. Between the two forks of the "Y" a wire is strung on which flat metal discs are suspended. When the sistrum is shaken, the metal discs create sound as they rub against each other.

Materials

- "Y" shaped branch
- Thin, easily bendable wire or cord
- Washers that have holes in them or pop tops from soda cans, paper clips, buttons, etc.
- *For teachers only:* Hammer and nails (if using bottle caps) or ice pick

Directions

1. Take a nature walk with your class. Look for Y-shaped branches that have fallen on the ground.
2. Back in the classroom, attach one end of the wire or cord to the top of one fork of the "Y" by twisting or tying.
3. String the metal washers (pop tops, buttons, paper clips, etc.) onto the unattached end of the cord or wire. If you are using bottle caps, you will have to create a hole in the middle of the cap. This can be done quickly by hitting a nail into it or pushing an ice pick through it. These caps can also be prepared by the teachers or aides at home and brought to the class strung or ready to be strung.
4. Tie or wrap the other end of the wire or cord to the other fork of the "Y."
5. Cut off the excess wire or cord.

Play the sistrum by holding it by the "tail" of the "Y" and shaking it.

Guiro

A guiro is a South American instrument made out of a long, dried, hollowed-out gourd. It is played by scraping a wood or metal stick over notches that have been cut into the gourd.

Materials

- Evian water bottle or any other plastic bottle with ridges
- Beans, rice, lentils, etc.
- One chopstick, ice cream stick, or pencil

Directions

1. Make sure the ridged plastic bottle is thoroughly air dried on the inside.
2. Put a small amount (about one-quarter cup) of dried beans, rice, peas, etc., into the bottle. Screw on the plastic lid.
3. Take the stick and scrape along the ridges to make sound.
4. The guiro may also be shaken or hit to produce different sounds.

Option: Either before or after the completion of your instrument, the outside may be decorated with paint, feathers, torn paper, or other materials.

Rainstick

Rainsticks are indigenous to Central and South America. Real rainsticks use dried and hollowed-out bamboo or cactus as the body. Nails are driven into the body in a spiral candy cane stripe pattern. Crushed shells or fine gravel are placed inside and the ends are sealed. Myths and legends tell of the rainstick being used by Indians to bring rain for the harvest or hung outside the village to scare away evil spirits.

The rainsticks students will make are simplified versions of the originals and do not necessitate any nails being inserted into the tube. (It is these nails in authentic rainsticks that inhibit the falling of the gravel and make the slow trickling sounds that mimic falling rain.)

Materials

- Long cardboard tubes from gift wrapping paper or, for shorter rainsticks, paper towel tubes
- Old newspaper
- Dried beans, lentils, rice, etc., or fine gravel like that used in an aquarium
- Masking tape
- Scissors
- Paint, feathers, glitter, glue, fabric for decoration

Directions

First Session

1. Take a sheet of newspaper and twist it tightly into a snake-like roll. It should not be loose and wide, but as narrow and tight as possible since it will loosen up inside the tube.

2. Cut the newspaper snake into a length somewhat longer than the tube you are using. Wrapping paper tubes will take an entire sheet or more.

3. Push the newspaper in this tight, twisted shape into the cardboard tube. If it becomes bent or crushed in the process, this is okay because it is the circuitous form inside the tube that will actually be more inhibiting to the trickling materials.

4. Tape one end shut with masking tape. Trim the excess roll of newspaper so it does not hang out of the open end more than four inches. This excess may be needed to control the speed of the trickling materials.

5. Choose materials or a combination of materials to place in the rainstick. Gradually pour a small amount into the opening, listening to the sound that is being created as it falls. If the beans or rice fall too quickly, take some of the excess newspaper and push it into the tube to create more of a blockage. If the materials are falling too slowly, pull the twisted newspaper a little straighter to allow things to fall more quickly. Do not overfill.

6. Seal the open end.

Second Session

Decorate the tubes with paint, feathers, glitter, or fabric. Set aside to dry.

Simple Drums

Materials

- Metal coffee cans with plastic lids
- Chopsticks or sticks of any kind
- Optional: Dried beans or rice

The simplest drums can be quite effective and may be played in three different ways. Although oatmeal boxes and other round cardboard boxes may be used, these will always have a rather dull sound. Metal coffee containers with plastic lids that fit snugly are great to use for small drums. Some of these also have ridges. By hitting the plastic lid with your hand or a stick, a surprisingly resonant tone can be produced. Scraping the metal ridged sides produces yet a different sound, as does hitting the metal bottom. Dried beans or rice may be placed in the can to give it another use as a shaker. The cans can be decorated.

Pan Lid Gongs

Students with enthusiastic parents may be able to get an old pan lid on loan from the kitchen. If it has a handle of some kind, so much the better. The best thing to hit it with is an old wooden spoon, a wooden stick, or a chopstick. Hitting with a metal spoon creates a rather loud and harsh sound. The pan lid gong is a welcome sound in the midst of homemade instruments, many of which are shaken.

Tiny Shakers

Find small plastic pill bottles or other small bottles and fill them (never more than a third of the way) with a fine material such as dried rice or aquarium gravel. These tiny shakers can be easily decorated after they are made and are easily held. They can also be strung and suspended for children who cannot hold or shake them.

Instruments for Children with Severe Disabilities

Suspended Instrument Rack

Find or create a metal rack three to four feet high and about three feet wide. From this rack, triangles, shakers, bells, tambourines, pan lids, drums, or other percussion instruments can be suspended.

Children who use wheelchairs and children with cerebral palsy or other neuromuscular disorders who do not have the strength or coordination to hold an instrument can produce sounds from these suspended instruments. The children can touch the shakers or tambourine and a sound will result. If a small drum is suspended, they can hit it with their hands. Jingle bells barely need to be touched to produce a sound. If a child can hold something light like a thin wooden or metal stick, he or she can create sound on a triangle or a suspended toy xylophone.

For children who are severely involved, this sound rack of suspended instruments can provide motivation and stimulation to make specific body movements, with the goal of creating sound. The sounds produced can provide immediate gratification, and children can be allowed to play with these sounds as they would with other recreational materials. Students in wheelchairs may be brought up to the rack. Semi-ambulatory students may be supported by an adult as they explore the sounds.

A less permanent, and perhaps less difficult, alternative is to suspend a sturdy cord such as clothesline from one side of the room to another. The instruments can be suspended on the clothesline. When the session is over, the clothesline may be taken down and the instruments put away.

Electronic Floor Pads

There are toy stores and some music resource catalogs where you can buy plastic covered pads that can be laid on the floor. Battery operated, these pads have electronic sound producing devices in between the plastic covers that are activated when pressed on in any way. Some models have been discontinued, but even so there are different versions of this pad available; you will have to ask about it specifically at various toy stores. One of the most common is in the configuration of a large piano keyboard designed to show the black and white keys. An earlier version that may still be available is a pad with colored circles. In either case, when the keys or colored pads are pressed, stepped on, or have any pressure put on them at all, they create a tone.

The good thing about these sound pads is that even a child with severe disabilities, who can only crawl, can have the experience of creating sound by merely touching random spots on the pad. In addition, since most instruments used in classrooms are percussion instruments, the use of high and low pitches from a scale in a different sounding (albeit electronic) timbre provides a new sound creation process and listening experience.

Other Options

Jingle bells, small shakers, or other instruments that make a sound when moved can be attached to children's wrists with straps or Velcro. You may also look for instruments that are designed for this purpose.

Music and Language

 ## Music, Language, and Rhythm

Music and language both have their own specific symbol systems and use sounds and silences moving through time as their medium of communication. The tone quality of voices speaking or instruments being played can reveal feelings and emotions in the speaker or player. In truth, almost all the principles of how sound changes in language are applicable to music as well. In both, sounds can be fast or slow, long or short, high or low, and loud or soft. Silences can be used to emphasize expression or delineate sections. In addition, both music and language have structure, and from the combination of sounds, silences, and structure emerges meaning.

Music has sometimes been called a universal language because it can transcend the cultural barriers of spoken words yet still communicate in such a way that human beings can respond both emotionally and kinesthetically. Language not only conveys and evokes emotion, it also can communicate thoughts and image ideas.

Language Skills and Beat Competency

The beat that is always present, if not audible, in all music originates with the beat of the human heart. It is a phenomenon that is as natural as it is comforting.

Beat competency, or the ability to hear, clap, play, or move in time to a steady beat, is one of the most basic musical skills for both teachers and students. This ability not only opens the way for higher order music skills, it also has been proven to be linked to a child's learning of spoken words.

This is not so mysterious as it is logical when one considers that music and language are both patterns of sound and silence moving through time. The organized subdivision of these longer and shorter sounds and silences within a measured beat creates what we will call "rhythm." When a child can anticipate (consciously or unconsciously) where the next beat will occur, each beat becomes an aural "signpost" for the temporal placement of music or word patterns. The same is true for moving to the beat of music.

As you use the sound and music activities, keep in mind that singing, clapping, playing, and moving in a variety of contexts provide excellent opportunities for honing the beat competency of both teachers and students.

Rhythm

In music, rhythm is the organization of longer and shorter durations of both sound and silence moving through time. Rhythm takes its life from the beat or pulse of the music. All rhythm relates back to that beat, just as all the voluntary and involuntary life rhythms in our body relate to the pulse and beat of our hearts. Like the beat of our hearts, the beat in music can vary in speed.

 ## Rhythms and Words

Throughout world traditions, the wedding of music and words has created songs and other vocal forms ranging from operatic arias and recitatives to contemporary urban rap songs. One key element linking the two is rhythm. All languages have their own sophisticated rhythms. It is the creative

94

exaggeration of the natural rhythm of language that is used in most vocal music forms. In some cultures, high and low pitches can actually change the meaning of a word. African and Asian cultures, among others, rely on high and low voice inflections to communicate specific meanings of some words in their languages. On the other hand, purely rhythmic patterns without any spoken words have, in some African traditions, become an actual language of pure sound and rhythm that can convey specific information as precisely as any spoken language.

There are many activities in which words, rhythms, and instrumental sounds can develop both musical and linguistic intelligence. After using some of the ideas in this section, try making up some of your own activities. Relate the subject matter to other areas you might be studying.

Tonal Competency

Prelinguistic vocalizations of babies, using pure vocal sounds but no words, are often attempts to imitate the inflections of human speech. Tone can be thought of as a sound that communicates meaning or intentions. Pitch is the highness or lowness of sound that assists in carrying that meaning, be it specific, as in language, or more abstractly aesthetic, as in some instrumental music.

Although this handbook offers more activities that are rhythmic and instrumental, it is not intended to detract from the importance of tonal competency: the ability to hear, learn, create, speak, sing, or replicate high or low pitches in various sound combinations, whether sung or played.

The Importance of Singing

Because spoken language skills can be helped by the development of beat and tonal competency, singing is one of the most accessible and valuable ways to assist learning in these three areas. Since most special needs teachers already use singing in the classroom, collecting (or creating) an "arsenal" of songs for a wide variety of occasions and purposes can increase the ways in which you use music as a powerful teaching tool. You may collect or create:

Songs for greeting or farewell	Songs about animals
Songs for counting	Songs for special occasions
Songs for movement	Songs that soothe and relax
Songs for identifying parts of the body	Songs that stimulate
Songs for acting out daily activities	Songs about feelings

Other ways to develop beat competency, tonal competency, and language through singing are

Singing songs	Moving to songs
Listening to songs	Clapping (etc.) to songs
Creating songs	Playing instruments with songs
Singing instead of talking	

Remember that replication, imitation, or "call and response" ways of singing with your class can be gamelike and fun. When children enjoy singing, or any other activity, they will welcome repetition, which in itself assists the learning process. You may discover that certain children who cannot or will not speak will be able to participate in and communicate through singing.

Language as a Source of Rhythm Ideas

Clapping or hitting drums or other simple percussion instruments in conjunction with word rhythms are effective ways to develop rudimentary rhythmic skills and awareness. These activities can also motivate the use of language in children who have difficulty speaking. Language can reinforce rhythmic awareness and rhythm can motivate the use of language.

The following two activities can have many variations. The first is a simple one-on-one exploration that uses language and rhythm in a dialogue-like exchange. The other takes the dialogue concept one step further by having two groups of children respond to one another, first using words, then words and rhythms, and finally rhythms alone.

Speaking and Playing Simple Phrases

Activity Process

Estimated Time: One session

Suggested Music: None

Level

Low to high functioning. Students should be able to clap hands or hit or shake a percussion instrument with hand or stick. The ability to speak their names or a simple phrase is a plus.

Benefits

- Fine and gross motor coordination
- Rudimentary rhythmic skill and perception
- Awareness of the rhythms inherent in spoken language
- Ability to use language as a source of rhythm ideas
- Communication skills through the medium of instrumental sound or the spoken word
- A sense of interaction and dialogue exchange
- Ability to replicate a sound or language rhythm

Considerations

If the children can hold an instrument and follow directions, they may use their own instruments. Otherwise, you may hold the drum while a child responds. A drumstick or mallet with a rubber or yarn head or a hand may be used to strike the drum. Clapping is an option. Although this does not have the excitement of playing an instrument, it is a clear sound source, a strong visceral experience for the clapper, and often a good warm-up before proceeding to the use of an instrument.

Materials

- One or two drums or simple percussion instruments whose sound is created by striking them

• Optional: One or two sticks or mallets

Directions

1. You may sit and address one student at a time and proceed through a progression of simple words or phrases, or you may have a small group of students sit in a semicircle, addressing each one individually and then proceeding to the next.

2. As you say "Hel-lo," hit the drum two times, one hit for each syllable.

3. Offer the drum to the first student and ask, "Can you say 'hello' to me?" Or, depending on the ability of the student, "Can you say 'hello' to me on the drum?" The responses, depending on students' comprehension, linguistic ability, and physical coordination, could range from

   A simple verbal "hello" with no drum hits, to

   An imitation of what you modeled (saying "hello" while simultaneously striking the drum on each syllable), to

   Hitting the drum two times with no speaking.

4. Following are some simple phrases that you may take in or out of order depending upon what your students can do. Speak slowly and clearly, and exaggerate the language rhythms. The procedure in this first round would be for you to model and then ask each child to

   Speak the words only (no drums) if language is a problem,

   Try to speak the words and hit the same rhythm on the drum as the words are spoken, and

   Hit the drum only if speaking is not possible.

   Bold syllables are to be given an accent, or sound emphasis, when spoken or played. Some children may naturally respond by speaking and playing while others will need suggestions and a modeling of their response. For example:

   "**Hel**lo **Dan**ny" Then ask, "Can you say 'hello' back to me?"

   "**My** name is Ms. **Mor**gan. **What** is **yours**?" If necessary, help them respond by explaining that they should say, for example, "**My** name is **John**-ny." (If you are working to develop language, encourage full statement responses rather than just a name.)

   "**How** are **you**?" A possible response is "I am fine."

5. These same phrases can be expanded upon using your own imagination and using subjects that might be applicable to your classroom. You might ask a question about the class's pet rabbit, Buster:

   "**How** man-y **ears** does Buster have?"

   Answer: "**Two**."

6. Vary the questions and answers, working with one or more children as the situation dictates.

7. If you are working with higher functioning students and have instruments available, you might have students try "talking" to each other in short phrases. Two cautionary thoughts: If every student with an instrument "talks" at the same time, sound chaos will ensue and nothing can be heard or appreciated. You can work with just two instruments at a time. Hand them out to two students at a time and have them perform

their spoken or played dialogue in front of their classmates. The process should be improvisatory, with no rehearsal necessary.

8. Addressing one student, "say" something by playing on the drum, but use no language, only rhythm. The student should be given a chance to respond, but this time the sound response will be totally free rhythmic expression without attached language. Imitation may occur naturally but should not be requested or expected unless you specifically want to use this phase of the activity to develop aural or musical replication skills.

What is important in this activity is the general process of using rhythm with instruments and relating it to exaggerated language rhythms. The specifics of what you "say," the way in which you work with your students (i.e., one-on-one or a group effort), and whether you put the emphasis on the musical or linguistic development is your choice.

Group Dialogues

This activity can stretch into many areas of learning, including creative writing. The idea is to emphasize that sound, either as music or language, has always been used for communication. A written dialogue can be developed by you or by the entire class based on a given scenario. That dialogue should then be spoken by the class, one group for each of the two parts. Using the process below, this written and spoken dialogue can be transformed into a musical, rhythmic dialogue between two groups of instruments.

Activity Process

Estimated Time: One session if you prepare the dialogue ahead of time; two or more sessions if students create the dialogue.

Suggested Music: None

Level

Most suitable for higher functioning students who can read, speak, and write and are physically coordinated. Students should have the ability to work together as a group, follow directions, and be able to hear the rhythms of spoken language as related to musical rhythms played on instruments.

Benefits

- Writing and speaking skills
- Fine and gross motor coordination
- Awareness of rhythms inherent in spoken language
- Ability to play and replicate rhythms on percussion instruments
- Ability to use language as a source of rhythm ideas
- Ability to work cooperatively as part of a group
- Ability to focus and follow directions

Materials

- Paper and pencil for writing down individual ideas
- Blackboard and chalk or poster board and magic marker for writing down final dialogue so that the whole class can see it

• One instrument per student (if there are not enough instruments, body sounds, found sounds, mouth, or vocal sounds may be used)

Directions

1. Give students a scenario with a problem. The scenario should be between two groups of people who must interact and communicate, through questions and responses, to find a solution to the problem. (An example of a specific scenario is given below.)

2. If students are not capable of writing individual ideas, you can try creating a dialogue as a class if time allows. The dialogue writing should take no more than one or two sessions if the class is involved. If you create the dialogue by yourself, it could be worked within the first session.

3. Transfer the dialogue onto the blackboard or onto one or two poster boards so that it can be read, and clearly delineate which part is for which group.

4. Following is a sample scenario that will illustrate the process:

   Scenario: Two villages lie on either side of a river. A man-eating tiger is on the loose and the people from both villages must communicate with each other so that they can capture the tiger and be out of danger.

Group 1 (speaks first)	**Group 2** (answers group 1)
1. Have you seen the tiger?	1. Yes! We've seen him.
2. Where is the tiger?	2. He's running over there.
3. Can you tell us where he lives?	3. He lives inside the cave.
4. Maybe we can catch him!	4. Then we can celebrate!

5. First have each group speak their lines, one at a time; group 1 speaks first. The first line of group 1's part should be answered by the first line of group 2 before group 1 goes onto the next line, and so forth.

6. Next, keeping a steady beat, exaggerate the word rhythms of each line. Come to an agreement as to how the rhythms of the words should be spoken. Following is a suggestion for accenting (emphasizing with sound) certain syllables of this dialogue.

Group 1 (speaks first)	**Group 2** (answers group 1)
HAVE you seen the **TI**-ger?	**YES!** We've **SEEN** him!
WHERE is the **TI**-ger?	**HE'S** running over **THERE**!
CAN you tell us where he **LIVES**?	**HE** lives inside the **CAVE**!
MAYbe we can **CATCH** him!	**THEN** we can **CEL**ebrate!

7. After the rhythm of each line and the appropriate accent are agreed upon, have each group, in turn, chant the words rhythmically, with the accents, back and forth, one line at a time. However, this time, each line should be said four times before the other group responds.

8. Do step 7 again, adding the clapping of hands in the same rhythms as the spoken words, clapping harder on the accented syllables. Each line should be done four times before going on.

9. Do each line of dialogue four times, as before, this time with the clapping of the rhythms and accents only. There should be no speaking.

10. Pass out instruments or settle on body, mouth, vocal, or found sounds for each person in each group.

11. Using instruments and sounds only, no words, play the original rhythms and accents of the dialogue that were previously spoken and clapped. Your dialogue has now become a musical dialogue.

Variation: By adding high and low pitches to the rhythmic words, a song can be created.

Many different rhythmic dialogues can be created from working with language. If students like this activity, have them bring in new dialogue ideas for the class to transform into music and rhythm.

Partner Sound Activities

These activities can be adapted to a group format if students are not equipped with the independence and other necessary abilities to work with a partner. It may depend on the adult/student ratio in your class.

Working with a partner concretizes the communication aspect of music as well as developing interpersonal awareness and sensitivity. It provides an opportunity to explore the various ways in which people can communicate with sound.

The following process, level, benefits, and materials apply to all three activities in this section.

Activity Process

Estimated Time: One session or part of one session

Suggested Music: None

Level

Students should be capable of working with a partner and physically able to play an instrument. Alternative sound sources may be used. If necessary, this activity may be done with a partner in a supervised group context.

Benefits

- Interpersonal sensitivity
- Expression and communication through sound
- Rudimentary rhythmic skill and perception
- Fine and gross motor coordination

Materials

Instruments or alternative sound sources for each student

Mood Duets

Warm-up

1. Use the "How Am I Feeling?" activity on page 88. (Your students will be using the vocal sound "Ah" with all possible sound changes to express an emotion.)

2. Stand in a circle with instruments after the "Ah" activity is finished. Go around the circle, one person at a time, and have them express an emotion on their instruments. You may limit the emotions to happiness, sadness, anger, and fear, or leave the choices to the student.

3. After each student has expressed an emotion, have others try to guess what it was.

101

Directions

Note: You may choose to go around the circle and be part of several twosomes yourself to model the following process.

1. Divide students into partners. If this is not possible because of ability level, the lack of adult assistance, or the amount of noise it would create, remain in the circle formation. If you do this, you will still have the students work with a partner, but you will supervise each twosome and work with one duo at a time while the rest of the class observes.

2. Have the partners face each other.

3. You may have each partner decide on a feeling or emotion ahead of time, and "talk" with his or her instrument to the partner, taking turns, in a dialogue fashion. Everything should be spontaneous and improvised. The important thing is that emotions are being expressed in the exchange.

4. As each partner duo does their "mood duet," the rest of the class watches. They may also be invited to guess what emotions have been expressed.

Variation: You may give each partner an opposite emotion or state of being such as happiness and sadness or caring and not caring. It is the job of one or both partners to try to convince the other, through sound exchanges only, to come around to their way of feeling.

Call and Response

This is a simple partnering activity that calls for imitation. One partner plays a pattern and the other repeats it exactly. This can continue until the imitating partner gets it right or until one partner has had several chances being the "caller." Then the roles can be reversed.

Call and response may also be done as a circle activity with one caller and the group responding.

Playing Together, Planned and Improvised

Dialogues have inherent structure in the taking of turns. When two people want to play together at the same time, it helps to have a structure to work with to prevent chaos, just as in any human interaction.

Warm-Ups 1

- Student 1 plays freely on an instrument and then stops, allowing the other student to respond, also freely.
- Student 2 responds and then stops to give the partner a turn.
- This process can continue as long as desired.

Note: The teacher may have to help stop one partner or prompt the other to respond.

Warm-Ups 2

- Student 1 plays one steady beat, over and over, then stops.
- Student 2 responds freely with anything he or she wants.
- Repeat steps 1 and 2 at least four times and change parts (i.e., student 2 plays one beat over and over and then stops, and student 1 responds freely).

Note: These warm-ups may be done using clapping instead of instruments at first.

Directions

One student should keep a steady beat while the other student plays freely in improvisatory style over that beat. For some students, it might help to concretize the musical element of a repetitive, steady beat by telling them to think the word "Yes" and play that on their instruments over and over (but without speaking it). In some cases, the teacher may have to keep the beat. But if the students can attempt to do this, it is an excellent opportunity to develop beat competency.

1. While student 1 plays "Yes, yes, yes, yes . . ." over and over in a steady beat, without speaking, student 2 will play freely over the beat.

2. Student 2 has two ways to approaching playing:

   Play in such a way that it helps student 1 keep the beat, or:

   Play in such a way that it makes it difficult for student 1 to keep the beat. (Sometimes this can be thought of, in fun, as trying to make your partner "mess up" his or her steady beat.)

   What is happening here is a structured, planned, unchanging musical part occurring simultaneously with an improvisatory, constantly changing part. When student 2 plays rhythms to "help" student 1 keep the beat, the rhythms will most likely be tamer and more regular than the rhythms student 2 will play when trying to cause his or her partner to lose the beat.

3. After this has been done, reverse parts and let student 2 (or the teacher) keep the steady beat while student 1 improvises to either help or hinder the beat keeping. Reversing parts continuously allows this activity to continue as long as desired. The signal for exchanging roles can be given by the teacher.

Rhythm Activities

Following are two short rhythmic activities that, although gamelike in spirit, can also serve as good warm-ups for other activities in sound and music.

Level

Students should have the ability to make minimal bodily movement of any kind. Students should also be able to play a short rhythmic pattern, or at least make a sound on their instruments and have the stamina to repeat this sound a number of times. If instruments are not available for all students, "found sounds," vocal, body, or mouth sounds can be used.

Benefits

- Following verbal instructions
- Working interactively with instruments (or other sound sources) in a group process
- Fine and gross motor coordination
- Making creative decisions involving bodily movements and rhythmic sound patterns
- Ability to hear and play rhythmic patterns
- Rudimentary perception of thick (many instruments playing) and thin (few instruments playing) sound textures

Rhythm Machine

This activity is similar to the "movement machine" in the Dance chapter. In addition to movement, sound will be used to create a living "machine" made up of students making sounds and, if possible, moving together. Please note that this activity also may be done with sound only, or movement only.

Activity Process

Estimated Time: One session or part of one session

Suggested Music: None, unless something is added with which the children would play after the machine has been created initially. The main focus should be on the sound and movements the students themselves create and how they fit together. If the activity is done with movement only and no instruments or other student-generated sound source, taped music of your choice may be used. Music with a strong sense of beat is recommended.

Materials

Instruments and alternate sound sources (body, vocal, found sounds) for students.

Directions

1. Have students stand in a circle facing the center with their instruments (or sound sources).

2. Go around the circle once and have everyone, one at a time, create a short rhythmic pattern or sound event.

3. Go around the circle again and have each person do the same thing, this time—if possible—adding a movement he or she they can do with the rhythm pattern or sound event.

4. Choose one student to be the central "hub" of the rhythm machine.

5. Have that student go to the center of the circle and make his or her sound and movement. This should continue repeatedly with occasional short rests, if necessary.

6. Either voluntarily, or as you choose them, have students go into the circle one at a time and "attach" themselves to anyone who has already joined the rhythm machine. They do not have to touch the person, just be beside him or her. Each student should make his or her sound and movement and repeat this to keep the energy of the machine going strong.

7. Continue this process until everyone in the class has joined the rhythm machine.

8. You may want to videotape or audiotape your rhythm machine. Photographs will not capture the sound element.

9. You may reverse the process and "decompose" the rhythm machine by having students leave the machine one at a time until only one student remains playing in the center of the circle.

Note: Step 2 might be to start with movement only. Sound could be added next.

Who's Left?

In addition to developing rhythmic skills and fine and gross motor coordination, this simple activity also provides opportunities for listening to thicker (many instruments playing) and thinner (fewer instruments playing) sound textures. It can also be used as a warm-up for other sound and music activities.

Before starting, explain that at some point everyone will be playing. Also explain that while everyone is playing, you will walk around and point to two students. Those two students will play along with everyone else, but when you give a big cutoff signal for everyone to stop playing, those two students chosen will continue to play. For visual and memory stimulation, you could put a piece of green ribbon draped or tied onto the two students as reminders to everyone that they will continue playing when everyone else is signaled to stop. (See "The Conductor's Gestures," page 107, and "Basic Gestures," page 107.)

Activity Process

Estimated Time: One session or part of one session

Suggested Music: None

Materials

Instruments and alternative sound sources for students. (See "Sound Sources for Your Music Activities," page 85).

Directions

1. Have all students stand (or sit, if standing is not possible) in a circle formation with their instruments, facing the center.

2. You or your aide can stand in the circle and begin to play a loud steady beat. You may also choose another student or two to help you play the steady beat.

3. After the steady beat is established, invite students, one by one, to join in playing whenever they want. If they can play a rhythm that "fits" with the beat in some way, that is good, but if not, simply playing will suffice. They should continue playing. (They may take a brief pause to rest, if necessary.)

4. Once everyone is playing and the beat is heard behind the many rhythms, walk around the circle, listening. Choose two players and point to them. You could have an aide attach the identifying green ribbons to the two chosen players. You may need to remind them that they must continue to play after you stop everyone else.

5. Make eye contact with every student in the group. Then, make a large cutoff signal. Everyone should abruptly stop, while the two students you previously pointed to continue to play.

6. Pause while all students listen to the thinner texture, the timbres (sounds) of the two instruments, and the rhythms they are playing.

7. After a moment of silent listening (to the two players), make a large signal for everyone to resume playing. You may have to reinforce the beat at this point with arm gestures or by picking up your instrument again and playing the beat.

8. After the beat is heard and everyone is playing, walk around again and pick one, two, or three players. Point to them (remind them) so they will know to continue playing, and then cut everyone else off.

9. Listen to the results and repeat the above procedures as desired.

10. Pick a student to choose those who will remain playing. The student leader should be capable of giving a signal to the group to stop and start again.

These simple rhythm games create an exciting atmosphere in which working together produces immediate and stimulating sound rewards. The relative freedom of deciding what rhythms or sound events a student plays is balanced by the structure or game rules of each activity. The games are wonderful techniques for group dynamics. The children are relating to one another through pure sound and with a common goal. When and if the rhythms and beats "fit together," there is the added bonus of being part of a larger musical and rhythmic sound experience.

Conducting Warm-Ups and Activities

Conducting is a group activity that allows children to experience the roles of both leader and follower. As with many arts activities, what can be revealed to you as you watch your students go through this process may surprise you. When in the role of conductor, rambunctious, overly energetic children who have trouble following directions suddenly find a channel for their aggressive behavior that allows them to interact with their classmates in a positive leadership role. Likewise, these children, when in the role of musicians, are likely to follow the new conductor with great enthusiasm, having just experienced being a leader themselves. More shy, less confident children sometimes need to be urged to stand in front of a group. But once they do, the structure of the activity supports them.

For children who are musicians and sound makers, their eagerness to play their instruments makes them willing participants in a new and exciting game. Having a group structure, a few simple ground rules, and working as part of a whole creative process is almost always more satisfying than just playing randomly and "making noise" on an instrument.

The Roles of Creator, Player, and Listener

From a creative standpoint, all the children, whether conducting or playing, are also in the active roles of composer and musical improviser in a very rudimentary way. Everyone will have to make creative choices involving the use of sound. Before anything can happen, the conductor has to make some decisions. What instrument do I want to hear next? How long should it play? Do I want a lot of sounds to happen one after another very quickly? How many people do I want playing at one time? Players must decide how they will play their instruments and how they will respond to the conductor's cues. These are essentially some of the same questions composers and improvising musicians ask themselves.

Finding Sounds

Homemade instruments, class percussion, or even found sounds from home, outdoors, or your classroom make conducting and group playing activities special. (See "Sound Sources for Your Music Activities," page 85.) Although adults and teachers can understand that a child will respond with excitement to playing a drum, it is more difficult to understand why students become excited about shaking a coffee can containing paper clips. It is not just the novelty of using everyday objects to create sound for sound's sake. By playing in combination with other sounds, what comes out of the "instrument" becomes an aural, yet nonlinguistic expression, and consequently an extension of the child. Communication and interaction with others, as well as the release of physical and emotional energy, can occur without the commitment to or the fear of spoken language.

If you do not have any instruments—bought, made, or found—or if your children cannot hold or manipulate them, find any sound that a child can make. (See the list of "sound sources," page 85.) Perhaps the sound will be a hand slapped down on the tray of a wheelchair or the surface of a desk, a vocalized, "AAH!," a squeak, or a mouth sound such as, "Chh! Chh!"

The Conductor's Gestures

The conductor will make two basic gestures: one to start playing and one to stop playing. Since you will probably model these, except where students are high functioning enough to create their own appropriate gestures, you may want to practice them yourself. The conductor may use a baton if desired. If so, a single chopstick, an unsharpened pencil, or any other stick six to eight inches long will work well in this capacity. It is not as important to define vocabulary words (see "Music Glossary," page 124) such as "cue" or "cut off" as it is to understand how to respond appropriately to the visual gestures for them—that is, unless language is an area that you would like to use all opportunities to develop.

Basic Gestures

1. A *cue* is a signal to begin playing. Cue to play: Point your finger (or baton) at a student. If you want two people to play music at the same time, point at them with one finger from each hand (or baton and fingers).

2. A *cut off* is a signal to stop playing. Cue to "cut off": (1) With one hand and arm make a downward, sideways slashing motion, or (2) cross both arms in front of you and quickly uncross them (in a slashing motion) to the sides.

Other Gestures

1. To continue playing: Beat up and down with one or both hands or make forward rolling motions with one or both hands.

2. To have more than two people play at a time: Point quickly at each person and move arms up and down in a beating movement.

3. To have everyone play together: Sweep or wave arm (with baton) from one end of group to the other and make up and down beating movements with one or both arms. Large forward rolling or waving movements indicate to keep the sound going.

4. To play loudly: Make very large gestures of high and low beating movements or large forward rolling movements with both arms.

5. To play softly: Make very small beating movements with the hand or hands. Crouching down or hunching shoulders seem to help convey the idea of "soft." If conducting small movements with one hand, a finger to the lips in a gesture of "Shh" also conveys the idea of playing softly.

Warm-Ups and Activities

Because warm-ups will ease students into playing their instruments, responding appropriately to conducting gestures and cues, they should be first led by you. Students may then be invited to try leading one of the warm-ups.

These warm-ups explore the sounds of the instruments and allow students to practice following the simplest cues of starting and stopping. They can help develop the basic skills of playing together to a conducted beat and imitating a simple rhythm pattern.

Although the conducting activities that follow these warm-ups are described as being done with four to eight students at a time, plus one conductor, they are so basic that they may be done with the entire class in a circle formation.

Level

To be a conductor, students should be able to point fingers or gesture directionally with hands or arms. Being able to hold a conducting baton is optional. Students in the "orchestra" should be able to make sounds on a simple percussion instrument by hitting, shaking, or scraping them. If instruments are not available, they should be able to do this with "found sounds" or make sounds with their bodies, voices, or mouths. Playing students should also have the cognitive ability to mentally process and respond to a visual cue by the conductor.

Benefits

- Fine and gross motor coordination
- Leadership and the positive channeling of unfocused or aggressive behavior
- Following directions
- Cognition of and response to visual hand signals in relation to sound-making on an instrument (body, etc.)
- Musical perception in the area of timbre (sound color), rhythm, sequence, and patterns of sounds
- Making creative choices using sound
- Developing basic musical skills of beat competency, rhythm replication, etc.
- Increasing vocabulary

Materials

Instruments and alternative sound sources, including hands for clapping.

Activity Process

Estimated Time: One session. This activity may be repeated in any number of succeeding sessions with different results every time. It is also a good idea to give as many students as possible a chance to conduct.

Suggested Music: None

All that is needed are instruments or alternative sound sources for each child. Again, it is strongly suggested that you model the conductor's role first. For many students, conducting will be an entirely new experience. Once they see how it is done, they will pick up on it quickly and enthusiastically.

If you have a larger class (more than eight to ten students), you may want to have one conductor and six to eight "musicians" up front. Students can then take turns as conductor and players.

Depending on the size of your class and their ability to follow directions, you may want to work with the entire class in a circle formation. Adapt the following processes to whatever physical structure works for you.

Exploration of Timbre (the distinct sound color of different instruments)

The primary purpose of this activity is to raise students' perceptual awareness of all the different sounds that are being played. The secondary purpose is to direct students' attention to how the sounds are produced.

1. Have everyone stand in a circle, with you as conductor also in the circle.

2. One person at a time in the circle will demonstrate his or her sound. Use your cuing gesture to indicate that you want them to play.

3. Ask different groups of instruments to play:

   All instruments that make sounds by being shaken

   All instruments that make sounds by being struck

   All instruments that make sounds by being scraped

   All instruments made of plastic, wood, metal, etc.

4. You may also work on meanings of words like "shake," "scrape," "hit," "wood," "metal," and instrument names.

Personal Expression

1. Ask each person in the circle to say his or her name. Have the students repeat their names again, and as they say them, play their instruments. You may want to have your own instrument handy to demonstrate. Ideally, you should say your name, and as you say it, play the instrument simultaneously in the same rhythm as your name. "Susan" would be two hits (or shakes). Some students may only be able to say their names and make a sound that is rhythmically unrelated.

2. Go around the circle and ask each person to play his or her instrument in a happy, sad, or angry way. Have the rest of the group guess what emotion the player is trying to communicate.

3. Ask students the following questions at the appropriate time:

   How is sad playing different than happy playing? Which is faster? Which is slower?

   How is angry playing different from happy playing? Is it louder or softer?

   Ask other questions that are relevant to students' playing.

4. Create other sound activities or variations on these ideas that let students freely express themselves on their instruments (see "Mood Duets" activity, page 101).

Sound Change Explorations/Stopping and Starting

These exercises in loud, soft, fast, and slow sounds are group sound explorations of some of the ways sound changes in music. No attempt need be made to play in a specific rhythm unless you have the ability and desire to accomplish this. What is important at this stage is for the children to have the experience of playing and hearing loud and soft, fast and slow sounds.

Depending on the creative flow, you may let a student conductor take over and try some of these ideas with the group. It may be that things are going so well that at any point in the warm-up you can ease into using student conductors.

1. Make a big gesture with both hands to indicate that everyone should play.

2. Make a cutoff signal and have everyone stop.

3. Have everyone play loudly by making a big starting gesture and making big continuous motions (this will create a lot of sound in your room).

4. Cut off and have everyone stop.

5. Put your fingers to your lips and make a small gesture signaling everyone to play softly. Keep motioning for students to play softly until you make a cutoff gesture.

6. If you can, indicate to everyone to continue playing with your beat. Create a fast beat. Create a slow beat. Cut off and have everyone stop.

Beat and Stop

The "Conducting Ideas" focus on student responses to cues, sound changes in music, and sequencing of sounds, one after another. This activity also requires that the students focus eyes, ears, and body awareness on you, the leader. It introduces the idea of clapping or playing a beat together, in unison, and stopping on cue.

It might be best to do this gamelike activity first with clapping, after which instrument playing may be substituted.

Directions

As the leader, you can impart a mischievous sense of fun in the process.

1. Hold your hands up in front of you, palms facing students.

2. Instruct students to do the same. Everyone is now ready, holding this "pose."

3. Explain that you are going to clap three times. Students should watch and listen and try to clap exactly with you.

4. Slowly and carefully, clap three times as the students clap with you. On the third and last clap, have your hands "rebound" into your original starting position, palms facing students. Students should be doing the same.

5. You may announce how many beats you will be clapping when you repeat this. It could be three again, four, five, two, or one, etc., depending on the students and their ability to count, coordinate, and follow directions.

With this process, the students will know ahead of time how many claps to expect. They are not only practicing counting and body coordination but reinforcing their beat competency under close guidance. Therefore it is important that the beat you clap is steady and even.

Variations for Higher Functioning Students

1. You may say, "Now I'm going to clap and I want you to clap exactly with me, but I'm not going to tell you how many times I will clap. Maybe I will clap one time, maybe three times, but I'm not telling—you must watch and listen closely to clap with me."

   Slowly and carefully clap in a steady beat with no counting. Your last clap will be the rebound "cutoff" clap that returns your hands to the starting position of palms facing students.

   This variation provides a sense of challenge and fun for students since there are no linguistic clues to help them. As always, a sense of fun and unthreatening "challenge" can help motivate students to sharply focus eyes, ears, and body movements on the leader.

2. Substitute instruments for clapping in all the "beat and stop" activities.

3. Choose students who understand the process and are successfully clapping and stopping to be the leader.

4. Optional: Work in two teams. When clapping (or playing) without counting is done successfully, everyone stops together. However, if someone "hits" a sound after the final group clap, that person must sit down. The team with the most people remaining standing after a designated number of "wins." **Note**: It is suggested to do this as a

team exercise only when there is an exceptionally positive and supportive class chemistry, lest those who must sit down feel "shamed."

Imitation

1. Play a simple rhythm.
2. Ask who can imitate it.
3. Ask the whole class to imitate it in unison.
4. Ask a student to make up a simple, short rhythm.
5. Ask another student to imitate it.
6. Ask the whole class to imitate it in unison.
7. Continue this process as long as you wish.
8. To get a feeling of "call and response" in your imitating activities, you may model the leader's role before choosing a student to take the lead. You create a short rhythmic pattern. Play it alone (the call) and have the group play it back to you in unison (the response). (You may need to lead the responses as well.) You may try playing this one pattern a total of four times as a call. After each call, have the group respond by echoing your call. After doing this activity four times with one pattern, change to another pattern. You may vary the length and difficulty of your rhythmic pattern. When students understand the leader's role and the group's role, you may pick a student leader to give the call.

More Conducting Activities

You may use the full circle or have the entire class sit down except for the chosen conductor and a smaller group of musicians.

It is advisable to begin by modeling some of the simple ideas suggested below. Each conductor will then create his or her own unique "piece" based on the creative combination of these ideas. All directions should be as physical, visual, and nonverbal as possible, unless using speech is a priority. There may be times when verbal clarification will be necessary.

Activity Process

Estimated Time: One session. This activity may be repeated in any number of succeeding sessions with different results every time. It is also a good idea to give as many students as possible a chance to conduct.

Suggested Music: None

Before formally beginning the conducting, it is a good idea to have each student try out his or her instrument. (The preceding "circle warm-ups" can also serve this purpose.) If a student can come up with a short rhythm to play, so much the better. If not, just a sound is fine.

Conducting Ideas

You will probably model these activities before choosing student conductors. You may use words or create your own gestures or use those suggested.

1. Choose one student to play.
2. Choose different students in different orders.
3. Go around the circle one at a time, giving each student in the circle a chance to play.

4. Reverse directions, each student playing one at a time.

5. Have two people play at one time, then three people, four people, etc.

6. Have everyone play together and then cut off.

7. Using physical gestures, ask the group or individual to play loudly or softly.

8. Using physical gestures, ask the group or individual to play fast or slow.

9. Starting with one student playing, have that student continue and gradually add one person at a time until four, six, or the entire group are playing together.

10. With the entire class playing, cut off one person at a time until only one student is left playing.

11. Cue four people in a row, one after another, to play in order. Their instruments might be a maraca, a drum, sticks, and a triangle. Having created a sequence of sounds, repeat that sequence a number of times. There is now a pattern of sounds.

12. Reverse the sequence and create a new pattern: triangle, sticks, drum, maraca. Point to each person in sequence and repeat this pattern a number of times. (**Note:** If the students want to create these patterns, it will help to do it with players who are standing next or fairly close to each other in line or in a circle.)

Conducting a Simple "ABA" Music Form

Form is a plan that organizes musical ideas into a specific sequence or arrangement. A theme in music is a main idea that usually recurs in various ways in a piece of music. With spontaneous conducting ideas, you can demonstrate a simple **ABA** piece to your students. Some of them may catch on and try it.

Idea A
Sequence of sounds: Drum, triangle, sticks

Repeat **Idea A** four times: Drum, triangle, sticks
                                Drum, triangle, sticks
                                Drum, triangle, sticks
                                Drum, triangle, sticks

Idea B
The conductor uses any of the previous "Conducting Ideas" (page 111) in any combinaton.

Idea A
The sequence of sounds (drums, triangle, sticks) is repeated four times as in original idea "**A**."

As in dance, by adding one more sound idea ("**C**") , a rondo form can be created (**ABACA**). Unless your students are higher functioning and you want to begin writing these forms on the board, the **ABA** form is probably enough for student conductors to be able to create while working under your guidance and with their own creativity.

With this idea of "form," two things occur. First, simple sound sequences become part of a larger piece of music. Second, students expand their understanding of pattern and sequence in a more complex sound plan.

Conducting activities can be implemented on different days with students in the different roles of conductor, player, or listener. If you have a dynamic conductor and a cooperative group of players, they can create a collaborative improvised piece that can be suitable as a musical performance in itself. The audience will not only be hearing a final product but will be able to observe the process of creative decision-making in the conductor's directives and in the sound and rhythmic responses of the players.

Simple Sound Activities (For Severely Involved and Lower Functioning Students)

It is common in a class of children who are severely involved, autistic, or multiply disabled to find that the majority of their musical activities consists of singing or using percussion instruments to play along with children's song tapes. For teachers without a music background, this is one of the safest ways to expose children to music. These activities are of value in developing beat competency and tonal competency as well as other aural skills, linguistic abilities, fine and gross motor coordination, rhythmic acuity, and interpersonal group participation.

However, there are other ways to work with sound that are so basic, simple, and obvious that they are often overlooked by many teachers, with or without a music background. These activities are not so much an artistic use of music as they are a creative use of sound to activate, stimulate, and motivate students.

"One, Two, Three"

This is a simple exercise that can be easily expanded upon with ease. It deals with reading and saying numbers and being able to play (or clap) a specific number of beats on a percussion instrument.

Activity Process

> *Estimated Time:* One session in which you may go as far as you can. Reinforcement is very positive in follow-up sessions where you can review what was learned, use additional numbers, and create different ways of having students play them.
>
> *Suggested Music:* None

Level

Very young and lower functioning students who are learning to count and who have the ability to clap or make a sound on a percussion instrument. This activity works best with small groups of attentive students who can follow directions. If the latter is not the case, extra adult help can make things workable. Students should be familiar with the numbers 1, 2, and 3.

Benefits

- Fine and gross motor coordination
- Sound perception of instrumental timbre
- Cognition of numbers of beats and combined patterns of beats being played
- Rudimentary mathematical abilities
- Counting

Materials

- Percussion instruments or hands to clap with
- Three large cards (or sets of these cards) with the numbers 1, 2, and 3, each on a separate card in a different color (More cards and numbers may be used according to your students' abilities.)

Directions

You will be exploring numbers one at a time with individual students through playing an instrument.

1. Have students sit in a small semicircle. Each student should have an instrument he or she can hit or shake. (For students who can do it, hitting is easier to coordinate for playing and counting specific numbers of beats.) If there is no instrument, clapping can be substituted. In a small group, students may share your instrument, which you can hold for them if necessary.

2. Hold up a card with the number 1. Ask what number it is. Who can say it? Who can play it on their instruments? If no one can, you can model it by beating once on your instrument.

3. After you or one of the students have done this, let others have a turn, one at a time. If a child persists in hitting more than once, take his or her instrument and hold yours in front of him or her. After the student has hit it once, take it away. Hand-over-hand work also helps control beating an instrument. You may also clap for children who lack coordination or the ability to follow directions.

4. Follow the same procedure for the numbers 2 and 3. Thoroughly explore each number with each student individually. You may go beyond the numbers 1, 2, and 3 in any of these exercises if your students are capable.

Variation 1: Number Sequences, Different Children

This variation allows children to hear different numbers of beats in different combinations. To make it less demanding at this stage, one child should play one number of beats and another child the next number of beats. You can hold the card in front of the child you would like to have play.

1. Hold up the card with 1 on it. Have one child play it.

2. Next, hold up the card with 2 and have another child play it. You may take volunteers or call on specific children.

3. Try alternating back and forth in different combinations with a different child playing each number: 1,2 | 1,1 | 2,2 | 2,1, etc.

4. Try the same idea, adding the number 3. Alternate between 1 and 3, then 2 and 3. Try alternating among 1, 2, and 3 in different combinations: 1,2,3 | 3,2,1 | 2,1,3, etc.

Variation 2: Number Sequences, Same Child

This variation allows individual children to differentiate between numbers and attempt to play those numbers of beats on their instruments. For those children who can identify the number and say it but cannot play it, hand-over-hand work will reinforce the number they can recognize with the visceral experience of playing it.

1. Hold up one number and have one child play it. Try to give individual children a chance to play sequences of numbers of beats.

2. If your students are good at following directions, you may put cards with 1, 2, and 3 next to each other and use a pointer to indicate how many beats a child should play.

3. You may mix having one child and other children participate in hitting their instruments in various beat sequences.

Variation 3: Replication and Identification

1. Play one beat. Go around the circle and have each child replicate the beat on his or her instrument, playing it back to you. Do the same with two beats and three beats.

2. Try this again. This time put out the cards. As you play one beat and a child responds with one beat, have another child pick the card with 1 written on it. Another way to do this is to give each child three cards, with 1, 2, or 3 written on them. When you play one beat, have students each pick the proper card with the 1 on it.

3. Older or slightly higher functioning students may divide up with partners. They can show their partners a card with the number 3 and the partner will play three beats. If the playing partner gets it right, he or she gets to hold up a card for the other partner, who will play that number of beats on his or her instrument.

Variation 4: Symbol Substitution

Note: This process can and should precede use of numerical symbols when working with younger students or those whose cognitive abilities necessitate more primal representations of numerical values. These symbols, if necessary, may be preceded by physical objects such as blocks, balls, and fruit to help concretize the concepts of quantity in relation to numbers.

1. Create cards with dots, colored circles, or other geometric shapes instead of numbers. For example, one card will have one large dot. The next will have two large dots, the next three large dots, and so forth.

2. All of the previous procedures can be adapted for use with visual symbols instead of numbers. These may be used to reinforce numerical understanding by relating the symbols to the numbers, the speaking of the numbers, or the playing or clapping of the numbers of beats using any of the preceding suggestions as guides.

Other Considerations

1. If you are working with language, reinforce the speaking or counting of the numbers in the early stages of the activity.

2. If you have a musical background or are secure in keeping a beat, you may try leading the students in striking one beat together. It may be a little sloppy, especially if you are short on adult assistance, but if students have the ability to try it, it can break the tedium of waiting for turns.

3. Thre are many possibilities for increasing the complexity of numbers in various combinations (such as a card with two dots plus a card with three dots), as well as more complex number combinations (such as two plus one plus three).

Sound "Hide and Seek"

Activity Process

Estimated Time: One session. The game can go on as long as you wish.

Suggested Music: None

Level

This simple game is excellent for stimulating and motivating lower functioning children who are lethargic or find difficulty relating to the world around them.

Benefits

- Aural perception
- Motivation to relate to physical environment
- Spatial perception based on aural cues
- Physical movement with a specific goal

Materials

Instruments or other sound sources.

Directions

Note: These instructions presume that one or more adult facilitators will be present to assist.

1. Take an instrument that has a distinctive sound and play it for the class. An instrument such as a drum, triangle, tambourine, bell, or shaker has a sound that can stimulate a response and that children will recognize as something that is special. If your sound possibilities do not include an instrument, you may use a funny mouth sound or a "found sound" from your classroom (such as a can with paper clips in it that can be shaken).

2. Explain that you are going to hide and "bet" that students won't be able to find you. Select one student to be the "seeker."

3. Have everyone cover their eyes and instruct them not to peek. (You may also use scarves to tie loosely over their eyes.) You (or an aide) can then hide somewhere in the room (in a closet, under a desk, outside in the hall by the open classroom door, etc.).

4. The person who is hiding should then make a sound on the instrument, fairly loudly. You or your assistant can then release the child who was picked to find the "hider." That child will then begin looking for you. If he or she hesitates or has trouble, the hider should play the sound again until he or she is discovered.

5. After doing this a few times with different students looking for you, you may help other students do the hiding and playing of the sound while another student looks for them.

Guess the Instrument

For this activity you will need three instruments with distinctly different sounds. Good combinations are a triangle, a maraca, and a drum; a tambourine, a maraca, and a drum; and two sticks, a triangle, and a drum. The goal of this activity is to identify which instrument is being played by its timbre (sound color) alone, without seeing it.

Activity Process

Estimated Time: One session or more

Suggested Music: None

Level

Lower functioning students with aural cognitive abilities. Students do not have to be able to play an instrument, only to hear it and to be able to indicate verbally or by pointing the instrument from which they think the sound came. This exercise can work well for some autistic children.

Benefits

- Aural perception of instrumental timbre
- Cognition of sound as it relates to a specific instrument
- Linguistic skills in speaking an instrument name
- Visual cognition of the pictorial representation, if used, of an instrument as it relates to a sound being played
- Reading the written name of an instrument (expanded version)

Materials

- Three contrasting instruments (others for backup and substitution if desired)
- A cloth or a large piece of poster board

For the "Musical Quiz Show" (Expanded Version)

- Pictures (simply drawn) of the instruments with the instrument's name at the bottom of each picture
- Optional: A small stage or a suspended curtain (cloth). A microphone attached to a small speaker or karaoke box.

Simple Version of Guess the Instrument

The simple process of this activity works well for children who can or cannot speak but have cognitive aural or visual abilities.

Directions

1. Have children sit as close as possible to the instruments.
2. Demonstrate the sound of each of the three instruments, one at a time. You may choose a student to do this.
3. Line up the instruments on the floor or table behind a suspended cloth, or prop the poster board up in front of the instruments so they cannot be seen. (Students or aides may hold the cloth or poster board if necessary.)
4. From behind the cover, play one instrument.
5. Expose all three instruments and ask who can guess which was being played. If a child cannot speak the name of the instrument, have him or her point. Repeat the process using another instrument.

As a positive reinforcement for guessing the correct instrument, that student could be allowed to choose and play the instrument for the next round of guessing.

Expanded Version of Guess the Instrument: "Musical Quiz Show"

This version is for higher functioning students who have the ability to speak or are in the process of learning how to speak or read even single words. This process is an abstraction of the previous version because it requires that the listener be able to relate the sound to the pictorial or word representation of the actual instrument. These students should be able to match the sound of an instrument to a picture of that instrument and/or the written name of the instrument.

If you want to make this a real game, you can use a quiz show format. The process is almost the same. The difference is that the instruments (after their initial demonstration) are concealed behind the "curtain" on the "stage" you have created. In front of the stage you can have posted one or three pieces of paper with three drawn representations of the instruments. You could do them yourself with simple line drawings in magic marker—for example, a triangle, a maraca, and a drum in their basic shape. Underneath each, print the name of the instrument in large letters. (You may also opt to have drawings and words on separate sheets, thereby isolating the pictorial symbols from the words.)

Directions

1. To add an element of fun, pretend you are the master of ceremonies. Each "contestant" can speak into a microphone if one is available. Each contestant has a chance to guess which mystery instrument is being played.

2. As before, demonstrate each instrument and conceal it behind the curtain.

3. Call the first contestant to the front of the room. Using the (optional) microphone, ask the contestant to speak his or her name. (The idea of this version is to motivate speaking in addition to the timbral cognition.)

4. Play the "mystery instrument" from behind the curtain.

5. Ask the contestant to point to which of the displayed pictures (or names of the instruments) he or she thinks it was.

6. If the tambourine was played and the contestant points to the correct picture of the tambourine, have him or her say the name of the instrument into the microphone as you point to the printed word or the picture.

7. Each contestant gets three chances to guess which of the three instruments was played. Encourage positive reinforcement from the "audience" by clapping and having them join you as the contestant gets the right answer. Show the real instrument and let the contestant play it.

8. Repeat with another contestant.

By formalizing this process into the game show format, participation also becomes an opportunity for individual recognition by providing an opportunity for each child to be the center of attention in a positive way. These fantasy scenarios actually become momentarily real for some children, and as a result motivation to speak and respond can be increased.

Drawing to Music

This could be classified as a visual arts activity. However, the focus should be on listening to the music and responding to it by putting lines, shapes, and colors on paper. Without specific directions, the children should be able to express themselves freely in the visual arts medium of choice. Colored pencils, crayons, and magic markers are relatively easy to manipulate and require little preparation or cleanup.

Similar to the activity in dance called "free dance" where children are simply allowed to respond to music by using their bodies, this activity allows a "visual arts" response to musical and visual stimuli. Because it does not demand much from the student other than participation in the process, it is a good release activity to insert between more structured or tiring activities.

Activity Process

Estimated Time: One session

Suggested Music: You may want to play some of your own or your students' favorite pieces.

If you would like music that is not orchestral but has a rhythmic or dance feel, repeated patterns of sound and a steady beat, African, some world music, and some minimalist music could serve this purpose. Native American music is slow, with repeated patterns. Some African music is faster, with repeated rhythmic patterns. Reggae music is also rhythmically stimulating, with an upbeat, positive feeling to it.

Following are some suggestions for music from the Western European orchestral tradition that have a subtle or obvious connection to imagery:

- *Night on Bald Mountain* by Modeste Mussorgsky (fast)
- 1st Movement of Symphony No. 6 (*Pastoral*) by Ludwig Van Beethoven (moderately fast)
- *The Ride of the Valkyries* by Richard Wagner (moderately fast)
- *The Four Seasons* by Antonio Vivaldi (slow and fast)
- *Afternoon of a Faun* by Claude Debussy (slow)
- *La Mer* by Claude Debussy

Following are suggestions from the same tradition: beautiful distinctive pieces but with no intended imagery attached.

- 4th Movement of Symphony No. 40 in G Minor by Wolfgang Amadeus Mozart (fast)
- *Gymnopedie* by Erik Satie (slow) (piano solo or orchestral)
- *Waltz Serenade* by Peter Ilitch Tchaikovsky (moderately slow)
- 4th Movement of Symphony No. 7 by Ludwig van Beethoven (fast)
- 2nd Movement of Concerto for Flute and Harp in C Major by Wolfgang Amadeus Mozart (slow)

Jazz and music from various word cultures can work effectively in the previous drawing activities. With African music, Native American music, or minimalist modern music, repetitive sound patterns provide an opportunity for the creation of visual patterns. Although this may or may not occur, observation of your students' responses can be revealing in the way different students perceive and respond to music.

Level

Appropriate for most levels. Students should be able to hear music and hold a crayon or some other visual arts material to make marks on a page.

Benefits

- Aural perception
- Emotional response to music

- Fine motor coordination
- Expression of aural perception through a visual arts medium.

Materials

- White or other color paper
- Crayons, colored magic markers, or colored pencils; paints, fingerpaints, or other appropriate medium
- Tapes or CDs of various kinds of music (see "Visual Arts Music Appendix," page 153)

Directions

1. Have your students sit at their desks with their visual arts materials and paper.

2. Play a piece of music and let them respond to it on their paper. Remind students to really listen.

   What colors does it make them want to use?

   How does the music move: fast or slow, smoothly or jerkily?

   Does it make them want to draw smooth curving lines or straight angular lines?

   Is it loud or soft?

   How does it make them feel?

   Does it make them see a picture or story in their minds?

3. After students have completed their sound drawings, post all the pictures together on the wall.

4. Pass out another sheet of paper to each student and put on a piece of music that contrasts strongly to the first piece. (This difference could be fast and slow, agitated and calm, etc.) Have students respond to the new piece of music.

5. When students have finished these sound drawings, post them on the opposite wall.

6. Ask students if there are any differences in the overall "look" of the pictures. If so, how are they different? In color? In line contour? In shapes created?

7. You may play the first piece of music and ask your students to observe the pictures that were drawn with that music in mind. Allow students to make comments or point out any picture where they see a connection between it and what they are hearing. Do the same thing with the second piece of music.

8. One variation on the reflective part of this activity is to place all pictures on the same wall. Have students try to guess which picture was drawn to which piece of music. You may or may not play one of the pieces during the guessing time. Each child can then verify which piece of music his or her picture was based on.

Simple Drum Talk

This version gives special consideration to working with very low functioning students who have minimal language abilities.

Activity Process

Estimated Time: One session

Suggested Music: None

Level

Students should be able to hold a drumstick or mallet or, if not, be able to hit the drum with their hands.

Benefits

- Nonverbal communication
- Verbal communication
- Perception of language in relation to rhythm
- Motivation to speak or create sound on the drum
- Fine to gross motor coordination
- Emotional expression through playing an instrument
- Sense of interpersonal dialogue exchange (taking turns)
- Following directions

Materials

- One drum
- Two mallets or drumsticks (one for you, one for the student). A mallet is a stick with a yarn or rubber ball at the end. It produces a rounder and somewhat less harsh sound than a wooden stick and is less destructive to the head of any drum if hard hitting should occur.

Directions

You may adapt and change any of these ideas to emphasize the development of verbal skills, physical coordination, or whatever might benefit a given student. Students can hold their own mallets, have them held hand-over-hand, or use their own hands to strike the drum.

1. With the drum, approach one student. The student should be holding a mallet if possible. Take a simple word like "hello." Say and play the word simultaneously (two drum hits, one for each syllable). Then offer the drum to the student so he or she can play or say "hello" in response.

   Options:

   You may progress this to taking turns exchanging "hellos" or other simple words (or phrases).

   You may also encourage responses based solely on playing or on speaking, according to a student's abilities or needs.

2. This next step may occur within the same session or in a following session. Expand the verbal and drum offering to include the child's name. Play and say "hello" and the student's name. For example, "Hello **Jo**-seph" could be four even beats with an accent and sound emphasis on "**Jo**."

   Some students may be able to say "hello" back to you with your name while playing the drum. Others may say "hello" but not play the drum. Others may play the drum in or out of the rhythm of the words and may not say anything.

3. Other ways to explore "talking" back and forth on the drum might be to:

a. Say a phrase like "**My** name is **Nan**cy" while simultaneously playing the same rhythms and accents of the words on the drum. See if the students can say back the same phrase with their names, hitting the drum at the same time, in the rhythm of the words.

b. Try imitation and replication. You can use one, two, or three simple beats or make up a short and simple rhythm. See if a child can replicate or imitate what you do. Experiment and gauge the ease or difficulty of what you play from what you perceive to be the child's cognitive level based on his or her response.

c. Try "free talk" on the drums, without words, taking turns. Hold the drum and hit it in a free and expressive way as though you are talking to the child. Let him or her respond. See if the student can sustain taking turns with you.

d. You may also try projecting emotion into your drum dialogues. Talking can be slow and sad, upbeat and happy, loud, fast and angry, etc. Note how the student responds to what you have played. Is he or she responding emotionally also? Is the student trying to replicate what you're doing? If so, how successful is he or she? Does the student demonstrate a sense of humor?

Besides being fun and stimulating, "talking" on the drum can give children a great deal of emotional and physical release when they are allowed to respond freely. Taking turns also develops interpersonal awareness. If you interact in this activity with sensitivity and perceptiveness, you can acquire a great deal of information about your students as you relate to them through sound. You will know more about their ability to replicate and create sound and language rhythms separately or together. You will discover whether they are less threatened expressing their feelings nonverbally than verbally. Each child's interpersonal skills will become more obvious as he or she responds to your playing. You will find who takes the lead by initiating new feelings and patterns of sound and who follows by attempting to imitate.

In these sound activities, please note that it might be helpful for lower functioning children to interact with you first in an intimate, one-on-one way before they do so with each other.

Moving to Music

Using all music resource lists from the Dance, Visual Arts, and Music chapters, choose pieces, play them, and have the students physically respond in any way that they can.

Certainly a march will have a different feeling, speed, and beat emphasis than a waltz. However, the idea is to listen to the music and let the body respond freely. In the dance section are movement suggestions, logistical considerations, and other creative ideas to which you can refer. However, do not limit your own creative ways of working with movement and music. If you can feel the speed of the beat and the rhythms of the music or hear the rise and fall of the melodic line, you can come up with your own movements to express them. Then you have what you need to bring even a rudimentary structure into the activity of moving to music.

Intimate Listening

This is an intimate one-on-one experience in which very severely challenged children can listen to sound. Students who cannot move, speak, or see might respond well to this experience. Choose an instrument, preferably something with a non-harsh, light, bell-like sound, such as a triangle, a single bell, the plucking of one prong of an African *mbira* or *kalimba* (thumb piano), a toy xylophone, or the tone of a recorder. Play this *gently* and *softly* into the child's ear at close range, taking care not to startle the child. You may also softly call out the child's name. Note any response such as the blinking of an eye, vocal emanations, or twitches in the body.

Sound Suggestions for Intimate Listening

- Nothing with a harsh percussive attack
- Rainstick
- African thumb piano (*kalimba* or *mbira*)
- Toy xylophones (stroked or touched gently)
- Finger cymbals (struck gently)
- Triangle (touched gently)
- Recorder (use only if you have good enough breath control to play a very quiet sound)
- Soothing vocal tones (singing, humming, etc.)

Sound Exploration

One of the best instruments for this kind of sound exploration is a small-sized rainstick. These are available at many new age stores, music stores, and stores that sell imports from other countries. You can also make your own (see page 91).Twelve- to eighteen-inch long rainsticks can be held by the children, alone or with help. The act of holding the rainstick upright and then turning it in the other direction will produce a trickling sound reminiscent of raindrops, wind blowing through leaves, or waves at the beach. This is a "nature sound" in its origin and perhaps it is partly this aspect that makes it so fascinating to the severely involved or autistic child. There is also the fact that, unlike striking a drum, triangle, or xylophone, the source of the sound is invisible and seems to come from nowhere, although the child will know the rainstick is the source.

Playing a song tape, which certainly can provide an upbeat or soothing atmosphere, is fine. However, simply sitting quietly, one-on-one, allowing the fascination of sound and vibration to be viscerally and aurally experienced is often overlooked as being too simple or of little value. If you feel you are not a musician and don't know how to play an instrument, remember, you are not playing a piece of music. You are, with the child, creating a beautiful sound.

Music Glossary

Accent. A way of emphasizing sound in a specific place in music, similar to the way a syllable might be accented in a given word. Giving a louder, more forceful quality to a sound than to other sounds around it.

Baton. A small stick sometimes held by a conductor to help him or her lead a group of musicians.

Beat. The steady pulse in music.

Conductor. The leader of a group of musicians.

Cue. A signal from the conductor to play.

Cut off. A signal from the conductor to stop playing.

Duet. A piece of music for two performers, or two performers playing or singing together.

Dynamics. The volume, or loudness or softness, of sound.

Form. The shape or plan of a piece of music created by organizing musical ideas into a specific arrangement or order. For example, idea "A" and idea "B" can be arranged to create "ABA," a popular musical form. Ideas "A," "B," and "C" can be organized as "A B A C A" to create a musical form called "rondo."

Guiro. An instrument of South American origin, made from a long, hollowed-out gourd. Notches are cut into the gourd, and metal or wooden sticks are scraped over these notches to create a sound .

Harmony. Two or more sounds being played or sung simultaneously.

Improvisation. Spontaneous and un-notated musical ideas being immediately played or sung.

March. A piece of music usually written for parades or military occasions. A march has the speed of a brisk walk and is countable usually in two or four. John Philip Sousa is a composer who wrote many marches.

Melody. The "tune" of a piece of music. The result of combining higher and lower pitches with longer and shorter durations of sound and silence (rhythm).

Ostinato. A short musical or rhythmic sound pattern that is repeated over and over.

Pattern. A relatively short sequence of musical events.

Percussion instrument. An instrument upon which sound is produced by hitting, scraping, shaking, tapping, or moving it.

Pitch. The highness or lowness of sound.

Quartet. A piece of music for four performers, or four performers playing or singing together.

Rainstick. A Native American instrument in which either bamboo or cactus is hollowed out and dried, then pierced with nails and filled with pebbles or shell fragments. When inverted, the sounds mimic falling rain.

Rhythm. The organization of longer and shorter durations of sound and silence over time.

Rondo. A musical form in which the main theme or section recurs in ABACA form.

Sequence. An arrangement of musical events in a specific order.

Sistrum. An African percussion instrument made from a Y-shaped stick. Between the Y sits a wire on which flat metal discs are suspended. When shaken, sound is produced as the discs rub against each other.

Solo. A piece of music for one performer, or one performer playing or singing alone.

Tempo. The rate of speed of a piece of music.

Texture. The "thickness" or "thinness" of an overall musical sound occurrence based on whether many or fewer instruments are playing at a given time.

Theme. The main idea in a piece of music that often returns more than once in its original or varied form.

Timbre. The distinctive "sound color" of a specific instrument or voice that gives it its own unique "sound personality."

Trio. A piece of music for three performers, or three performers playing or singing together.

Unison. Playing or singing exactly the same thing at the same time.

Waltz. A piece of music originally written for dancing. A waltz can be counted in cycles of three beats (1, 2, 3/1, 2, 3, etc.) and has a flowing, relaxed feel to it.

Music Bibliography

Bernstein, Leonard. *The Joy of Music.* New York: Simon & Schuster, 1959.

————. *The Unanswered Question (Six Talks at Harvard).* Cambridge, Mass. and London: Harvard University Press, 1976.

Choksy, Lois, Robert M. Abramson, Avon E. Gillespie, David Woods, and Frank York. *Teaching Music in the Twenty-First Century.* Englewood Cliffs, N.J.: Prentice Hall, 2001.

Eddy, Junius. *The Music Came from Deep Inside (A Story of Artists and Severely Handicapped Children).* New York: McGraw-Hill 1982.

Fiarotta, Noel, and Phyllis Sterling. *Music Crafts for Kids (The How-To Book of Music Discovery).* New York: Sterling, 1993.

Hawkinson, John, and Martha Faulkner. *Music and Instruments for Children.* Chicago: A. Whitman, 1969.

Haywood, Carolyn. *Eddie Makes Music.* New York: Morrow, 1957.

Komaiko, Leah. *I Like the Music.* New York: HarperTrophy, 1989.

Rudhyar, Dane. *The Magic of Tone and the Art of Music.* Boulder and London: Shambala, 1982.

Spencer, Cornellia. *How Art and Music Speak to Us.* New York: John Day, 1963.

CHAPTER FOUR

Visual Arts

Over the door of the sacred tipi, they painted the flaming rainbow. It took them all day to do this, and it was beautiful.

—Black Elk, Medicine Man

There is perhaps no other art form that so surely guarantees a lasting product as a result of the process as visual arts. Music fades to silence as vibrations die in the air. A dance disappears as movement dissolves to stillness. The emotional interactions of theater leave only a memory. But the visual arts produce a solid physical reality that reflects the vitality of the process that created it.

In visual arts, beautiful illusions are created. A line becomes a circle when it curves and meets its other end symmetrically. A circle is only a geometric shape until it is colored yellow and has rays radiating from its edges. Blue paint on paper magically transforms when a white cloud is painted over it.

The visual arts encourage working in both solitude and quiet collaboration, as well as helping students to see with both inner and outer eyes. They will make creative choices and meet the challenge of learning to use artists' tools to express their inner visions in the outer world. The experience of shaping clay or putting paint to paper can be a catalyst for unlocking emotion, during both the creative act and the perception of the final result.

Using Music with Visual Arts Activities

Whether working, playing, dancing, or painting, music has a unifying and enlivening effect. The introspective nature of the visual arts leaves the emotions and psyche free to respond to and to be inspired by music.

Mellow jazz ballads, or flowing folk music on a Celtic harp, hammered dulcimer, guitar, or lute, all work well as background music. Other good choices are classical or baroque music; cyclical, repetitive music such as Native American flute music; and some new age music and twentieth-century minimalist music by composers like Steve Reich or Philip Glass. Such music creates a calm but energized atmosphere conducive to working creatively in all visual arts media. Reggae and other light, upbeat music can enliven the working atmosphere when stimulation is needed.

Setting Up and Scheduling Time

Working on arts projects means covering tables and desks and laying out paints, brushes, water, paper towels, and other materials. It means making sure children's clothing is protected and, of course, restoring the classroom to its original order afterwards. In addition, many artworks must be stored with care. All of this requires extra time.

So, when planning visual arts activities, be sure to allow ample time for setting up and cleaning up. Try to arrange it so that the arts process takes two to three times longer than the set up and clean up time. This helps ensure that your activity will not have to be cut short.

When students use their imaginations and explore their own visual ideas, the process of turning the ideas into a reality can be thoroughly engrossing. Even children with severe disabilities have surprised classroom teachers and visiting artists with their incredible powers of concentration during an art project. Although survival instincts and sensory gratification certainly shape a large part of human behavior, the arts provide intrapersonal gratification that can result in total involvement.

 ## Materials and Supplies

Coverings for Tables and Desks

- Large, inexpensive, lightweight plastic dropcloths are available in hardware stores. These can be used on floors or tables in place of or in addition to newspapers.
- Old plastic tablecloths
- Large plastic garbage bags, cut open and laid flat
- Newspaper

Classroom Materials

Although each activity in this chapter has its own supply list, it may be a good idea to keep a supply of the following staples in your classroom:

- Masking tape
- Scotch tape
- One-inch strapping tape (extremely strong, translucent tape with fibers running lengthwise; available in other widths also, at hardware stores)
- Blunt-tipped scissors
- White glue
- Rubber cement
- Wax or plastic disposable cups
- Plastic containers
- Medium or large plastic garbage bags
- Old newspapers
- Pencils
- Rulers
- Paper towels
- Empty egg cartons
- Plastic squeeze bottles with pointed tips

Supplies for Teachers

- Sharp pointed scissors
- Hot glue guns (very effective but can burn very easily)
- X-Acto knives (single-bladed knives with the blade pointed at an angle; good for cutting foam core board, cardboard, poster board, etc.)

Clothing Protection: Smocks

A parent's worn-out shirt with the sleeves cut short makes an excellent smock. Smocks can be tagged with the student's name, hung up, washed, and reused. If aprons or other smocks are unavailable, plastic garbage bags with head and arm holes cut out are an alternative.

Paint

Many artists prefer to use acrylic paint in the classroom. Its advantages are that it does not crack and flake like tempera paint and has a brighter look. Its disadvantages are that it is a little more expensive and does not always wash out of clothing. You must balance aesthetic and practical considerations when choosing your materials. If you decide on acrylic paint, a recommended brand is Liquatex. Spilling can occur in any paint project. Old plastic squeeze bottles with pointed tips make the pouring process much more tidy. Styrofoam or cardboard egg cartons, as well as metal muffin tins, are excellent containers in which to put some of the paints your students will be using.

Collecting Things from Home

Piles of old newspaper can take up precious classroom space. Even so, you and your students might gradually bring in things from home for your project. Keeping the following items on hand can save a last-minute rush for materials and provide both practical and creative options for your activities: plastic containers, egg cartons, magazines, pieces of fabric, dried beans, and rice.

Allergic Reactions to Art Materials

During your visual arts activities, if you notice an increase in hyperactivity or any other perceptible physical changes in any of your students, it may be that they are having an allergic reaction to one or more of the art materials. Be watchful of their responses when in contact with paint, clay, glue, etc. If you suspect that there is a connection between a specific material and a child's hyperactivity (or other change in behavior), you may want to experiment with alternative materials and note the result. (Consult with the school nurse about a child's allergy.)

Making an Ocean Drum

The mechanics of putting the drum together and decorating the surface make this activity more a visual arts experience than a musical one. When finished, your ocean drums will be beautiful not only to look at but to listen to as well. They can also be of use in activities that involve stories, music, drama, and movement.

In all cultures, humankind's fascination with the sounds of nature has inspired the creation of musical instruments. One way primal peoples have manifested their awe for the forces of nature and the magical powers of sound has been to decorate their instruments with beads, paint, shells, feathers, and other natural adornments. There is a tribe of aborigines in New Guinea that keeps ornate ceremonial flutes in sacred shrines and brings them out only for specific rituals.

An authentic ocean drum is a round drum with two heads, one of which is made of clear plastic. Inside are hundreds of tiny metal balls. When the drum is tilted, the balls roll and vibrate against the inner surface of the heads. Depending on the angle, the vibration created can sound like the rush of a gentle tide or the roar of breaking waves.

The least expensive and most easily accessible material to use in making the body of an ocean drum is a pizza box. Although it is square, the surface area is ideal for decorating, and the sound of the materials rolling in the box is satisfying. This is a practical, if not entirely aesthetic, choice. If your students are able, the box's square shape can be changed to a more circular one by crushing the corners inward and taping around the body of the box, or even using papier-mâché to round it out.

Activity Process

Estimated Time: Two sessions or more

Suggested Music: New age music with nature sounds, Native American flute music, drum and percussion music from different cultures, *La Mer* (The Sea) by Claude Debussy. Use of music is optional.

Level

Expect that you and your aides will end up doing much of the folding and assembling of the pizza boxes. Medium to higher functioning students, depending on their motor skills, can participate by helping tape down the edges of the box. Lower functioning students can paint, decorate, fill, and play the finished drum.

Benefits

- Fine and gross motor coordination
- Spatial perception
- Imagination and visual sense of design
- Aural perception
- Perception of the relationship among shape, sound, and movement

130

Materials

- Flat, unassembled pizza boxes (small or medium-sized), available in bulk from a friendly pizza store
- One-inch strapping tape (available at hardware stores)
- Blunt-tipped scissors
- Liquatex acrylic paint or poster paint, brushes, water, containers
- Surface coverings (newspapers, plastic dropcloths, etc.)
- Smocks
- Sequins, sparkles, sparkle paint, shells, feathers, colored pipe cleaners, colored tissue paper, etc. (if available)
- White glue
- Fillings for the drum: peas, rice, chick peas, pebbles, marbles, etc. (smaller, rounder shapes sound and roll the best)

Preparation and Warm-Up

1. Listen to tapes or watch videos that have the sound of the ocean or rushing water.

2. If you have an ocean drum or have made your own model of one, demonstrate its sound by holding it flat in front of you and tilting it slightly in various directions. Note how the speed and angle of the movement affect the sound. If you are able to purchase a real ocean drum to show your class, the Remo Company manufactures both children's and professionally made ocean drums. They vary in size and are priced from approximately $25 to $65. Musical instrument stores, particularly percussion stores, and progressive children's toy stores should be able to order one for you if they do not have one in stock.

3. Have students bring in drum fillings from home; see materials list.

Special Considerations

There are two approaches to creating your ocean drum. Choose whichever suits you.

- The drum (box) may be assembled, a small amount of filling added, then sealed. This allows the decorating to be done in two sessions: first, painting of the box, and second, gluing on of additional decorations. Although this procedure eliminates having to leave one flap open (which would have to be sealed and painted over later), it does make the remaining process rather noisy.

- The other alternative is to assemble and tape the box except for one flap. After the decorating is completed and the filling put in, this flap could be sealed with tape and painted over.

Session 1

1. Help the students assemble the pizza boxes. To save time, you and your aides may want to assemble the boxes prior to the arts session. This is the time to decide whether to put filling in the boxes or wait until the end. If you put in filling, seal the boxes completely afterwards. If not, leave some kind of opening. Do not use too much filling. Less than half a cup is enough (see Step 4 in Session 2).

2. Use strapping tape to smooth and secure the corners and edges of the boxes. Students should be able to help with this according to their abilities.

3. Paint the boxes with acrylic (or other) paint. Let the children freely express themselves with color, lines, shapes, and patterns on the surface of the boxes. Set the boxes aside to dry.

Session 2

1. Finish decorating the ocean drums with sparkle, feathers, colored tissue, etc. If the drums are sealed, they may be set aside to dry.

2. If the drums have an open flap, and the final decorating has been done, you may set them aside while fillings are decided on.

3. Take one empty box or one dry box and experiment with the sounds of different fillings. Ask students whether rice sounds different from marbles rolling in the box, and how.

4. Be careful not to use too much filling. Start with very little and gradually increase the amount until the sound is satisfactory. Use just enough to create the sound each student wants. Sometimes less filling can create more sound.

5. After the filling procedure is complete, seal the flaps or openings with tape and decorate the boxes.

Follow-Up

1. After the ocean drums are completed (and dry!), have the students form a circle and hold their drums flat in front of them. Try being very still with no movement and no sound. (This may be difficult to do without some filling rolling around.)

2. Very gently tilt all the boxes at the same time. Make the sound of a quiet wave.

3. Tilt the boxes faster and at a greater angle to the floor. Make the sounds of waves crashing.

4. Give your class nonverbal hand cues for loud or soft and fast or slow playing, starting, and stopping. Use student "conductors" if possible.

5. Create a "wave" of sound around your circle by having one person at a time play in sequence. Reverse the "wave" of sound by having students play one at a time in the opposite direction. Create other sound games that explore loud and soft, few and many players, etc.

6. You may ask, "What other sounds in nature does the sound of your ocean drum remind you of?" "What about city sounds?"

7. Use your ocean drum for sound design in stories, plays, or musical activities. Have students write a story or play about the ocean that features the sound of their musical artwork.

Papier-Mâché

Animals have always fascinated children. The idea of creating one's own "pet" opens a door to many other learning experiences and activities that involve emotions and interpersonal relations as well.

Activity Process

Estimated Time: Three to four sessions

Suggested Music: Music or children's songs with animal sounds or themes, such as *Peter and the Wolf* by Serge Prokofiev, *Carnival of the Animals* by Camile Saint-Säens, or the Paul Winter Consort. Happy, upbeat music, such as reggae, is also appropriate.

Level

This activity is best for medium to higher functioning students, depending on your classroom help. Trying this activity with lower functioning students depends on your own judgment. There are teachers of severely involved students who will undertake, with the help of their paraprofessionals, using the hand-over-hand technique, doing complex arts projects with wonderful results. In reality, the adults are actually accomplishing the tasks, but at the same time they are intimately sharing the experience with the students with whom they are working.

Benefits

- Fine motor coordination

- Three-dimensional spatial visualization and perception

- Tactile and sensory perception (rough, smooth, soft, hard, wet, sticky, dry, etc.)

- Intrapersonal and interpersonal awareness (if the "pet" idea is used)

- Visual imagination

Materials

- Plastic or newspaper to cover the working area

- Old newspapers, torn into pieces about two-inches in diameter. (Also save some full sheets to use.)

- Boxes of tissues or some paper towels

- Masking tape (at least one roll per child if possible)

- Liquid starch (other options include wallpaper paste, which is perhaps the best and is available at hardware stores, or your own sticky mixture of approximately one-half cup of white glue mixed with one-half cup or more of water)

- Shallow pan, lid, or container for starch mixture

- Safety scissors

- Paint: acrylic, Liquatex brand

- Brushes

- Water

- Optional: pieces of felt or fabric (for ears, noses, and tongues), buttons or plastic "google" eyes, available at fabric, crafts, or arts supply stores

Preparation and Warm-Up

1. Ask students if they have ever wanted a pet of their own. If so, why, and what kind? Ask them, "What can a pet do for you?" "What can you do for your pet?"

2. If a student has a pet, have him or her describe it to the class. Perhaps the student has a story about the pet to share.

3. Visit an animal shelter, zoo, farm, or aquarium to see many different kinds of live animals.

4. Bring in illustrations (photographs or drawings) of animals. Post these pictures in the room to stimulate your students' visual imagination. Note the outstanding characteristics of different animals, their shapes and colors: snakes have no legs, rabbits have long ears, Dalmatians have black spots. Do not limit the class to domestic animals; also include wildlife.

5. Have students draw a picture of a real or imaginary animal they would like as a pet. If a student would like a dog, have him or her draw a picture of a dog. Depending on your students and your feelings about reality versus fantasy, you can encourage them to make a "realistically" colored dog or allow them the license to create a blue one. If a student needs more reality-based play, perhaps his or her dog should be brown or black. If another student needs to stimulate his or her imagination, perhaps his or her dog should be pink or purple. The result will reflect your choices.

For higher functioning classes and situations requiring strong adult assistance, students may choose the type of animal they would like to create for a "pet." Wildlife should be included. For classes with lower functioning students or less classroom help, it may be easier to limit the choice of pets to one or two types. In that way the directions and process will be simpler for all involved.

Session 1

1. Have students bunch up full or partial sheets of newspaper to create separate shapes, or "parts," for their animals, such as a head, body, legs, tail, snout, and ears. They should pay attention to the differences of these shapes on the different animals being represented. Have them wrap and secure the individual shapes with masking tape, then use the masking tape to attach the pieces together in the proper positions. Students should liberally crisscross and encircle the areas where the pieces attach with the tape many times to make them as strong as possible. (This first step may take an entire session, or more.)

2. Put the starch or wallpaper paste into a shallow pan. (Be sure the work area is covered.) Have the students then take their pretorn newspaper pieces and dredge them through the mixture. They should try to wipe off the excess paste so the pieces are not too wet.

3. Ask students to apply the pieces in an overlapping layer to cover the animal shape completely. Have them smooth and define the lines of the "animal" as much as possible and wipe off the excess paste. It is best to do one layer per session to allow for proper drying. Dampness between the layers will weaken the sculpture.

4. Set the sculptures aside to dry overnight. (You may have to wait another day before your next session.)

Session 2 or 3

1. Have the students apply another layer of papier-mâché onto the "pets," this time concentrating more on the actual shape of the tails, ears, trunks, muzzles, snouts, beaks, etc. They should reinforce the joints and refine the details of the form with the papier-mâché pieces as much as possible.

2. For smaller details like noses and eyes, shredded newspaper or tissues soaked in starch, paste, or glue can be used the same way as clay.

3. Set the pets aside to dry and harden.

4. If time permits, repeat the first three steps in one more session. The more layers there are, the stronger the sculpture will be.

Session 3 or 4

1. Have students paint a base coat of acrylic paint (which dries quickly) on their animals. Then they can add spots, stripes, rings, masks, or other imaginary markings. Other options include felt or fabric for ears, noses, tongues, and collars. Students may paint in the eyes or use black and white felt, buttons, beads, or plastic "google" eyes.

2. If time permits, the painting and final touches might need to be worked on over more than one session.

Follow-Up

Most simply, the papier-mâché animals may be put on display or taken home. However, if you've opted to use the "pet" idea, you can create other activities that explore a relationship with an imaginary pet.

1. Have the students name their pets.

2. Whether the pets are domestic or wild, have the students find out what they would eat, how many times a day they should be fed, etc. Share this information with the class.

3. Have students write or verbalize a story about their "pets." They should read or tell the story to the class.

4. Allow students to keep their pets with them in class for a week or so. They may even create beds for them. Allow a playtime, an imaginary feeding time, or a time when they might communicate with their pets or other pet owners in the class.

5. If you don't already have one, you might surprise your class with a live pet, such as a hamster or guinea pig. Let students share the responsibility of caring for their new, live pet.

Playing with Clay

Working with clay can be a fascinating tactile and visual experience for children with disabilities. Clay is exciting to shape, explore, and manipulate. Its form can be changed fairly easily, unlike lines or paint on paper, and the challenge of using clay exercises fine motor coordination in a way that leads to creative discovery, even if a finished product is not possible.

The very act of kneading clay and working with the hands in this way can actually release tension in some children. A pleasant and relaxed atmosphere can be created in which students may want to talk to one another about their work.

Some artists and teachers may worry that the necessary smallness of the clay forms and figures creates too great a demand on the fine motor coordination of lower functioning students. This can only be determined by the value that you, as the teacher, put on the creative process, and whether a very simple product is a worthwhile outcome.

Activity Process

Estimated Time: One session

Suggested Music: Free choice (see "Visual Arts Music Appendix" at the end of this chapter) or optional.

Level

All levels of students, including lower functioning and visually impaired. Students, however, must have the muscular strength to hold and squeeze clay.

Visually Impaired Students

Working with clay allows visually impaired students to use their sense of touch to explore, form, feel, and perceive shapes and surfaces without having to process their tactile experience functionally as they do in everyday life. Also, through creative and guided activities, the act of holding shapes, changing shapes, and noting how those shapes relate to one another can increase cognition of spacial concepts that might be too physically large or conceptually abstract to understand.

Benefits

- Fine motor coordination
- Recognition of shape, size, and placement of three-dimensional forms in space
- Tactile stimulation and perception
- Perception of the transformation of an abstract geometric form into a representational form (or vice versa)

Materials

You will need clay (see below), paper towels, both dry and damp, and plastic containers with secure lids for storage.

There are three basic types of clay. Choose whichever suits your needs or is most easily attainable:

1. Oil-based clay is very temperature sensitive and must be stored away from areas that are very warm or very cold. When cold, oil-based clay hardens and must be worked between the hands before it will soften. This will leave an oily residue and necessitate having paper towels and water on hand. If you have a sculpture made of oil-based clay and the temperature is very warm, it could droop and fall. This clay costs about $1.75 per pound compared with the $.20 per pound for natural earth clay.

2. Earth clays are usually red or white and can be purchased in powdered form from commercial dealers in 25-pound bags at about $.20 per pound. If using earth clay, students should keep moistening the hands or the clay with damp paper towels or they might become frustrated. White earth clay is somewhat denser than red and is better for sculpting.

3. Dough-like clay (homemade or the commercial "Play-Doh") is very spongy and resilient when moist. However, it can dry and harden rather quickly if exposed to air for too long. Store it tightly wrapped in plastic containers. If it dries out, it cannot easily be moistened and reused.

At the end of your activity period, no matter what kind of clay you are using, collect the excess, roll it into a ball, and place it in a plastic container with several damp paper towels to provide moisture. If necessary, a metal container lined with plastic can be used for storage.

Preparation and Warm-Up

Because of the nature of clay, the ambiguity between process and ever-changing product, and varying levels of student abilities, these warm-up exercises may be considered activities in and of themselves.

The Magic Ball

Magic is transformation. In this exercise students will learn to make a ball of clay and explore several possible ways to transform that ball.

Words and Concepts to Explore

- Round, flat
- Big, small
- Soft, hard
- In, out

Directions

1. Have students sculpt clay into one big ball using two hands, if possible, rather than one hand and a table surface. (Hand-over-hand assistance will help with severely involved students.)

   Have them look at or feel the ball they've made.

   Have them roll it on the table.

   Have them roll it to one other.

   They should understand what "round" is.

2. The clay should be placed on the table surface and made into a flat pancake. Students may pick it up, feel it, and look at it. They should understand what "flat" is. (**Note:** If making a round ball was a major effort, you may want to keep it round.)

3. Students will take a small piece of their clay "pancake" and roll it into a small ball. They will make a bigger ball out of a bigger piece of clay. Ask students to

   Look at them or feel them side by side. As them: "Which is big?" "Which is small?"

   Have them say the words *big* and *small.*

4. Have students push two balls into one piece of clay again. They will make three balls all the same size or make one big, one medium, and one small. Balls may be stacked with the biggest ball on the bottom and the smallest ball on the top. Ask them: "What does that look like?" "What does it feel like?"

The variations that students will be able to come up with for transforming the "magic ball" are endless. They can make a small container out of a larger piece of clay by rolling it into a ball and pushing a thumb into the center to create an indentation, then squeezing the sides thinner as the indentation grows larger. Soon they will have a "pinch pot" or small container. A smaller ball may be made with the leftover clay and placed in the "pot." Students can explore the concept of "in" and "out." If they choose to keep the containers, they can be decorated by making markings with the tip of a pencil or pushing sequins, pebbles, or buttons into the clay while it is still soft.

Other free play can include transforming clay forms into snake-like shapes, squares, etc. Animals or animal heads can be attempted. Students can try guessing what animals each other's clay figures are supposed to be.

Hatching a Baby Bird

Activity Process

Estimated Time: One or two sessions

Suggested Music: Free choice (see "Visual Arts Music Appendix" at the end of this chapter) or optional.

To prepare for this activity, bring in an egg and show it to the class. A chicken's egg should suffice. Note how an "egg shape" is different from a round ball.

In weeks or days preceding the actual arts activity, you may want to put pictures of birds up in the room, go for walks to see live birds, or look at pictures of birds in books.

Note that birds have feathers, wings for flying, and beaks. Try to find a bird's nest to show the class. Ask the students: "What else might a bird sit on beside a nest? A branch? A rock?" Have students bring in branches, rocks, or small boxes that could contain a homemade nest of dried grass or twigs.

Directions

1. Give each child a piece of clay large enough to form an egg somewhat larger than a chicken's egg.

2. Have students create an oval, egg shape with their clay, preferably using both hands in the process as opposed to a table surface.

3. Once everyone has created the egg shape, "share" the eggs with the class before moving on to the next step.

4. Have students squeeze and pull out a head shape at the narrower end of the egg. They should make a bit of a neck for the head of the bird. If something goes wrong, students can always start over again.

5. Once the head is done, students can pinch out a beak for the baby bird. Will the baby bird's mouth be open or closed?

6. Fingers or a pencil or other tool can be used to make the outlines of wings on each side. Some birds' wings will be closed. Others might be slightly open.

7. Have students pull out a tail from the larger, still rounded end of what was the egg.

8. The point of a pencil can be used to make eyes, nostrils, and markings for the texture of feathers.

9. Legs are optional. The baby clay birds will probably not balance on twig legs and may collapse on clay legs, so it is simpler and safer to have the baby birds in a "roosting" position, using branches, rocks, or small boxes filled with dried grass to set them on.

Collage

A *collage* is simply defined as an artistic composition created by affixing different materials such as photographs, pictures, paint, fabric, paper, sand, or string, to a flat surface. With collage, the creative possibilities are endless. The collage may have a theme or it may be "abstract," focusing on shapes, lines, patterns, textures, and colors. The process described in this activity should be easily adaptable to your students' needs and abilities. (See "Adaptations for Lower Functioning and Visually Impaired Students" on page 142.)

Perceiving Emotion in Ourselves and Others

Collages are very "theme-friendly." This particular collage will have human emotion as its subject. As usual, feel free to use any theme relevant to your current classroom objectives.

One of the most necessary life skills for human beings is the ability to be in touch with one's own emotions. A closely related, vital life skill is the ability to perceive the emotional states of others. This skill is necessary to interrelate with compassion and sensitivity and respond appropriately in a variety of emotionally charged situations.

Four of the most basic human emotions are sadness, happiness, anger, and fear. Each emotion has its own range of intensity. "Happy" could range from contented to ecstatic, "sad" from pensive to very depressed, "scared" from frightened to terrified, and "angry" from peeved to raging. There are also related gradations of feeling such as calm, excited, and bored. You can decide which emotions you and your students will work with in your collage.

The Universality of Human Emotion

Teaching with a multicultural perspective, as so many of us do now, we learn to appreciate the beautiful diversity of artistic expression from one culture to another. Latin dance differs from African, Chinese, Latin American, Middle Eastern, or American and European dance, yet all dances involve the joy and beauty of movement. Working with drama activities and stories from different cultures, we see different characters in different settings, but the human issues and conflicts are very similar, as are the human emotions that respond to each situation. If you wish, you may incorporate into your collage a global view of human emotions.

Making Choices

If you choose to make a collage with your class, using "emotion" as the theme, following are some options to consider:

1. Work with only one emotion as the subject of your collage.

2. Work with the four basic emotions. Incorporate them into a single collage or create four smaller collages (one for each emotion). They may be displayed together or at separate locations in the classroom.

3. Use photos with faces only, or include body language.

4. If it suits your students' needs and abilities, you may choose to work with gradations of feeling such as calm, excited, moody, or pensive.

5. Create your collage from a global perspective and show the range of emotions from a variety of cultures. (This option may be determined by the photo and picture resources available to you and your students.)

Making a collage, like most of the other activities in this handbook, suggests a theme that can reach easily into other areas of learning. Your creative collaboration with these ideas will be the adaptations and refinements you make to suit the needs and abilities of your students as well as your own teaching goals. Feel free to follow the process for creating a collage, changing the theme if you wish, or make it simply an arts activity that emphasizes shape, color, texture, and composition.

Activity Process

Estimated Time: One to two sessions

Suggested Music: Classical, jazz, new age (see "Visual Arts Music Appendix" at the end of this chapter). If using a global theme, music from various cultures. Use of music is optional.

Level

Collage making will work with lower to higher functioning students, depending on process adaptations and the amount of classroom assistance you have. Unlike some other activities, the process can be adapted, to a certain degree, to the level of your students' abilities.

Benefits

- Fine motor coordination
- Spatial perception
- Recognition of emotion, based on visual information, as it relates both to oneself and others
- Visual imagination
- Tactile stimulation and perception
- Working in collaboration as a team; making group decisions

Materials

- Old magazines with lots of "people" pictures, such as *People, Life,* or *National Geographic,*or pre-extracted pages of photos of people
- Photos of students themselves, donated by students' families
- Color comic books
- Some newspaper photos
- Foamcore board (other options: cardboard, thick poster board, thin plywood, or any sturdy surface for your collage, sized to your needs)
- X-Acto knife (teachers only, for sizing foamcore board or other needs)
- Blunt-tipped scissors (for teachers, teachers' aides, and some students)
- White glue or rubber cement
- Optional: Paint (acrylic), brushes, colored tissue paper, yarn, and any other materials to enhance the collage

Preparation and Warm-Up

You could call the collage project "Our Feelings" or "A World of Feelings," depending on your theme and approach. Using the following simple steps as a guide, determine how and to what degree your students can participate.

1. If students can read, write the words describing various emotions on small pieces of paper: *sad, happy, angry, scared* (and others if appropriate). Fold the papers so that the "emotion" word is on the inside. Put the "emotions" into a can, hat, or other container. Choose as many students as there are pieces of paper to come up and pick one from the container. They should then line up in front, facing the class. (If students cannot read, you can tell them what emotion they picked, or eliminate the paper and whisper the emotions in their ears.)

The emotion should be kept secret. One at a time, the students in the line will portray, on their faces only, the emotions they have chosen. The class has three chances to guess what each emotion is. After someone guesses correctly, the next person in the line does the same with his or her "secret" emotion.

Depending on the parameters you have set for your collage theme, you may choose another group of students to re-pick the secret emotions from the container and portray the feelings through frozen "body language" poses. You may also pick two students to work together with each emotion and have them pantomime emotions in the context of interrelating. Variations can include giving one student one emotion and the partner a different emotion. No sound or movement is allowed. The class must guess the emotions.

There are infinite variations on this that could even include team games. These warm-up exercises will help focus the students on their preliminary task of identifying and categorizing photographs by the emotions they perceive in them.

2. Encourage students to bring in photos and magazines from home. (It should be made clear which, if any, photos may be used in the collage. Perhaps an explanatory note should go home with your students.)

3. Have the class look at photos of people expressing different emotions. Have them identify those emotions according to their own interpretations and discuss their opinions with the class. Questions to ask include: "Why does this person look happy?" "What makes that person seem sad?" "Is it his or her expression? Body language? The way he or she seems to be relating to another person in the picture?" "What could be happening in this picture?"

Teachers may use this process as a generic guide to creating a collage. Older and higher functioning students may participate in searching for, and extracting, appropriate photos. Others may work from pretorn pages or pictures you and your aides have chosen ahead of time.

Directions

1. Find illustrations that depict the range of emotions chosen for use in the collage.

2. Extract those pictures by tearing or cutting them out.

3. Identify and separate pictures into different "emotional" categories.

4. Make general decisions about the layout of the collage. Will the collage express only one emotion, or will it incorporate others? Should the different emotions be in separate areas of one collage or mixed together? Will there be a separate collage made for each emotion?

5. Decide if any words will be used in the collage.

6. Select larger or more striking pictures and decide where they will be placed.

7. After general placement decisions have been made, have students begin the process of gluing the pictures to a flat surface. White glue is easy to work with but can cause wrinkling. Rubber cement should be applied to both surface areas for optimal results and can easily be rubbed off should any leak onto the pictures.

8. After the pictures are glued on, students may add borders, paint, words, fabric, yarn, or other decorations.

You may also have students create collages of images or objects that make them feel, for example, "happy" (flowers, ice cream cones, Santa Claus, etc.), or some of these images could be integrated into the original collage.

Adaptations for Lower Functioning and Visually Impaired Students

Lower functioning students, for whom even the cognition of basic emotion is difficult, might have an easier time with a more concrete collage theme such as flowers, insects, animals, or holidays. They will still have the opportunity to identify many different visual symbols and representations that relate to one subject. Another possibility is to work with a more abstract design, focusing on color, shape, texture, and form. If you are teaching geometric shapes, students could work on a collage based on circles, triangles,or squares. Colors and numbers are other ideas to integrate creatively.

Teachers may still use old magazines and pictures as a major resource for this type of collage. The pictures, rather than being used for their image, can be torn into pieces so that the colors and shapes of the illustrations become the expressive material rather than the original picture itself. This can create a unique palette of colors and shapes that can be affixed to a surface background. Other materials (paint and three-dimensional objects) can be used as well.

Visually impaired students differ greatly in what they are able to see. For these students a textural collage can give a creative focus to their highly developed sense of touch. It can also allow them to make creative choices in how they group or juxtapose textures, in much the same way other students would make visually oriented decisions about spatial placement of figures or forms in a collage. In the same manner that you collected illustrations, collect and have students bring in materials that have distinctly different textures: sand, satin ribbon, wire screen, plastic, corrugated cardboard, Styrofoam, dried beans, rice, coarse fabric, slippery fabric, etc. Let students explore these textures and shapes and then create collages that will challenge and stimulate their tactile sense away from the practical context of day to day life.

Other Collage Themes

Add other collage ideas to the following themes:

- Holidays and special occasions
- Music
- "Our class"
- Dance
- Family relationships
- Folktales or fairytales
- "My special friend" or "friendship"
- Weather
- Different world cultures
- Urban or rural environments

Drum Painting

The experience of painting need not be limited to those who can manipulate a paintbrush. Even students whose physical abilities prevent them from using a brush to paint specific shapes or figures can create painted color forms on paper with the same energy and motion used to create sound on a drum.

Activity Process

Estimated Time: One session

Suggested Music: None at the beginning. Background music can be a distraction for students since they will be listening as well as looking.

Level

Especially good for mentally and/or physically lower functioning students. Also for mildly visually impaired students. Severely involved children may need to work hand-over-hand with an adult.

Benefits

- Fine and/or gross motor coordination
- Auditory and visual sensory stimulation
- Perception of the relationship between sound, movement, energy, color, and visual shape or patterns
- Motivation for movement with a specific goal in mind

Materials

- Smocks or larger bibs or aprons
- Substantial floor and table coverings
- Plastic containers with water
- Paper towels
- Thin strips of cloth (or cloth and scissors)
- Rubber bands
- Masking tape
- Clay (optional)—a small quantity
- Egg cartons or muffin tins for paints
- Paint (water colors or less permanent paint than acrylic might be best)
- White or light colored paper, 8 1/2 by 11 inches or larger depending on the size of the drum, or white or light colored thin cloth cut into round, square, or rectangular shapes (cloth may work better than paper)
- A drum or tambourine, preferably an old one, and the larger the better. (Perhaps one could be borrowed from the music teacher.)
- Ideally, old xylophone mallets with yarn heads. Rubber or wooden heads can always be wrapped with a softer material and held with a rubber band. If mallets are not available, try wooden drumsticks, wooden dowels, or strong sticks collected from outside.

Set Up and Materials Considerations

This activity can create paint splattering. Smocks for yourself and students, as well as substantial floor and table coverings, will save cleanup time later on.

The drumstick your students will use must have some kind of "head" to give it the weight that will create a sound when it strikes the drum. The head will also provide a surface area for absorbing enough paint to leave a colorful mark on the paper. Mallets with round rubber heads can be wrapped with thin strips of cloth, which can be secured with tape or rubber bands. Regular wooden drumsticks, wooden dowels, or other sticks can have clay heads stuck on them, then wrapped with strips of cloth. Or you can build up a head on the end of a stick by wrapping cloth and rubber bands around it. The weight of the head creates a sound when it strikes the drum and also absorbs an adequate amount of paint to make a mark on the paper.

Preparation and Warm-Up

1. Before you begin this activity, introduce the drum(s) to your students. Let the children try producing a sound on the drum, first with only their hands. With your hand, model playing one beat, two beats, three beats. See if students can imitate the number of beats you play using their hands.

2. Try a simple rhythm pattern. Who can imitate it?

3. Try a dialogue (taking turns playing).

4. Say and play words or names with drum rhythms, accenting the proper syllables. The words can be repeated (*JÓ-se Gon-ZA-lez, JÓ-se Gon-ZA-lez*).

5. Have students practice hitting the drum with a drumstick. Depending on the motor abilities of different children, the previous exercises can be more difficult with a stick. If so, only practice holding the stick and hitting the drum.

Words and Energy Qualities to Explore

- Drum
- Drumstick
- Sound
- Loud, soft
- Fast, slow
- Hard, light (as relating to a quality of energy, not a tactile or visual sensation)
- Numbers and counting
- Colors and color names

Directions

This activity requires practically one-on-one supervision and is best suited to smaller classes with substantial adult assistance. Depending on this and other logistics (the number of drums, drumsticks, students' abilities, etc.), decide whether one student or several students can participate simultaneously. Even severely involved students can enjoy this process with hand-over-hand assistance. The motivational aspects of the sound and visual stimulus are strong, and the movements are fairly simple.

1. Place a sheet of white or light colored paper or cloth over the head of the drum. You may want to tape it lightly in place at the edges.

2. Have a student dip the drumstick head in paint and "play the drum" lightly on the paper or cloth. Color forms and patterns will emerge on the paper or cloth from the same energy movement used to create sound.

Variations

1. Try hitting the drum one, two, or three times.

2. Experiment with changing colors. (You may have to have one drumstick for red, one for yellow, etc., or try rinsing the heads before changing colors.)

3. Hit the drum loudly (hard), then softly (lightly). Listen to the difference in sound. Look at the differences in the ways the paint creates shapes on the paper.

4. You and a student (or two students) can have a two-color "dialogue" on the same drum, "talking" back and forth.

5. Try playing simple rhythm patterns on different parts of the paper. Does the paint design repeat itself visually as the sound patterns do aurally?

6. If you work with emotions, such as happy, angry, or sad, you might ask a student to pick a color that seems cheerful or relates to his or her concept of "happy." Then ask the student to play the drum in a "happy" way.

7. Try making an "angry" drum painting. Ask students: "What colors reflect the feeling 'angry'?" "Does hitting the drum in an angry way create a louder or softer sound?" "What about the shapes the paint creates on the paper?" "Are they more spread out or more contained?"

8. You can have students work with all the ranges of emotion, relating feeling to quality of movement energy, color, resulting color forms, and sound qualities.

Other Ways of Using Paints with Lower Functioning Students

Twig Painting

Go on a nature walk and collect many different sizes and shapes of twigs. Soak them in water overnight. Students can grasp the twigs, dip them in paint, and explore lines and designs they can create on paper with larger, free arm movements.

String Painting

Materials

- 12- to 18-inch lengths of string
- White or light colored construction paper
- Paint of your choice
- Metal or plastic spoons

Have students fold a piece of construction paper in half. Ask them to open the paper and lay the string inside with enough hanging out so that it can be grasped and pulled. They should then squeeze a small amount of paint onto the paper. (They can use spoons to do this.) Have them use just one or several different colors. Have students close the paper over the paint and string. Students should then press the paper with one hand and drag the string out with the other hand. Ask students to open the construction paper and look at their string paintings. They can add another color and repeat the process.

Bead Painting

Materials

- An empty cereal box or other box approximately 8 1/2 by 11 inches by 2 1/2 inches
- White or light colored construction paper
- Paint of your choice in a variety of colors
- Scotch tape
- Plastic spoons
- Blunt-tipped scissors (unless used by teacher)
- Beads from old necklaces (other options are ball bearings, round dried legumes like peas or chickpeas, and marbles)

Ask students to cut a flap in the box by detaching three edges of one of the largest sides of the box. Have the smaller end remain closed, taping it if necessary. Students should then raise the large flap and place an appropriately sized paper flat into the box. Have students spoon or squeeze a small quantity of paint into the center of the paper. Then ask them to add a small number of beads (chick peas, marbles, ball bearings, or any other small round object). Have students close the flap. Holding the flap closed (or temporarily taping it closed), they should tilt and rotate the box. Students can hear and feel the movement of the beads as they roll around inside. Ask students to open the flap and look at the design that has been created. If students are happy with their paintings, they may be removed to dry. Students may add another color and repeat the process.

Some students do not have to have fine motor coordination to hold a paintbrush and experience the joy of paint and color. Hands and fingers have always been options for working with paints for all levels of students. Leaves and other objects from nature can be used as well. Expand your repertoire for ideas on working with paint by opening your imagination to all possibilities.

Rainforest Animal Masks

The mask has been a tradition in the rituals of music, dance, and storytelling throughout the world for centuries. Native American, Eastern Indian, African, Asian, and other cultures have made masks that represent deities or other mythical beings. Animal spirits have also been the inspiration for the masks or facial decorations of primal cultures that live close to nature.

Using the idea of rainforest animals for your mask allows outgrowth areas of study in geography and ecology. You may want to study the masks of one particular culture or use as models the animals of a geographical area other than the rainforest. Whatever you decide, you and your class will be able to use your masks in many ways, from enhancing storytelling and role-playing to being simple but beautiful wall decorations.

Activity Process

Estimated Time: Three to four sessions (one to two sessions using simplified process)

Suggested Music: Music with outdoor or jungle sounds, soundtracks of jungle movies, South American music and drumming (see the "Visual Arts Music Appendix" at the end of this chapter). Music is optional.

Level

Almost all levels, depending on simplified adaptations and classroom help available.

Benefits

- Fine motor coordination
- Spatial perception, judgment, and making aesthetic choices for placement of features in a face
- Tactile sense (textural variations of surface and materials used)
- Visual imagination

Materials

- White paper plates (plastic, Styrofoam, or "cardboard"; stronger plates if plaster gauze is used)
- White glue
- Wood tongue depressors (available at surgical supply stores or some pharmacies)
- Optional: Popsicle sticks, or other flat, narrow strips of wood, such as old rulers or paint stirrers
- Masking tape
- Stapler
- Blunt-tipped scissors
- Pencils
- Acrylic paint
- Brushes
- Water, plastic containers
- Paper towels
- Plaster-impregnated gauze (available at art supply stores). Rigid Wrap (by Activa) comes in a 4-inch-by-15-foot roll for approximately $3; Pariscraft (by Hunt-Bienfang) comes in a 20 pound box for approximately $55.
- Collected objects from home such as jar lids, yogurt containers, small cereal boxes, paper or Styrofoam cups, and ping pong balls (or any other lightweight, three-dimensional objects that will give your mask the contour of basic facial features before plaster gauze is applied)
- Decorative objects: pipe cleaners, yarn, fabric, felt, feathers, twigs, bits of fur—anything for details of facial features.

Preparation and Warm-Up

1. Have students collect and bring in objects from home or from nature that they might be able to use in their masks.
2. Study the masks of other cultures for ideas.
3. Explain to the class what rainforests are, where they are located, how they provide oxygen for the planet and homes and habitats for many people and forms of wildlife, and how they are being destroyed. (If you are not using the rainforest theme, familiarize your students with the culture or geographical region being studied.)

4. Have students find pictures of rainforests and rainforest animals. View them as a class and post them around the room. Teach the names of some of the animals and a little about them. Note the animals' colors, shapes, and other (especially facial) characteristics. Ask students: "Do they have a muzzle or a beak? Fur or feathers?"

5. Ask students: "If you could be an animal [of the rainforest or whatever geographical region you are studying], what animal would you be, and why?" "Do you identify with any of the characteristics of a particular animal?"

6. Give each student a plain, thin paper plate and a pencil. Have students practice the spatial placement of eyes, a nose, a mouth, and ears. At first, this may seem simplistic and unnecessary. However, many children, when asked to place facial features on any area like a paper plate, will "scrunch" them up into a tiny area in the middle of the plate. By previewing the placement of the features for the mask, students will have a clearer picture of where to tape objects for eyes, noses, etc.

The methods of mask making are as numerous as there are cultures in the world and ideas in the human imagination. However, using paper plates or cardboard, plastic, or Styrofoam as the basis for these masks allows a complex procedure to be simplified for lower functioning students. (See "Adaptation of Mask Making for Lower Functioning Students" on page 149.) These "seed" ideas will become your own when you freely adapt and refine any aspect of them to better suit your students' needs.

Remember that hand-over-hand work and other close adult help and supervision can allow a lower functioning student to experience a more complex process and, consequently, a more sophisticated art product.

If you are making masks with three-dimensional objects (as facial features) and using plaster-impregnated gauze, heavier plates would be best. If you choose the simplified process for lower functioning students, the most basic white paper plate should suffice.

Session 1

1. If you want to have a handle for the masks, have students take the tongue depressor (popsicle stick, etc.) and tape it two or so inches into the outer edge of the plate, allowing enough of the leftover "handle" to be comfortably grasped. You may want to cut two short horizontal slits near the edge of the plate and slip the handle through the slots to make it more secure before taping it in place.

2. With a pencil, have students lightly mark where the eyes, ears, mouth, nose, etc. will be on the plate.

3. Ask students to use masking tape to fasten the three-dimensional objects they have chosen for the facial features onto the plate. A yogurt container taped to the middle could be a rudimentary muzzle or snout. Small jar lids could be eye sockets. Ears could be two triangular pieces of cardboard. These objects will help give the mask its basic contours. Decorative three-dimensional objects such as yarn and feathers would not be added until the last session.

4. Help students cut the plaster-impregnated gauze into strips of varying lengths approximately one inch wide. Have them dip each strip in water before you begin to work with it.

5. Ask students to wrap the mask and taped objects in the gauze strips. Work in each strip by hand, rubbing it to "wake up" the plaster. The plaster will then become gooey and can be manipulated to make the surface of the mask smoother. If the plaster begins to become firm, as it does fairly soon, it may be moistened slightly.

6. Have students reinforce the attachment of the handle to the plate with gauze strips.

7. Set the masks aside to dry and harden.

Session 2

1. Ideally, this is a session for more plastering with gauze strips to refine the features and surface area. (However, if time is a problem or sufficient plastering was done in Session 1, you could skip to the painting in Session 3.)

2. If necessary, have students reinforce the attachment of the handle to the plate.

Session 3

1. Ask students to paint the masks with the basic colors of their choice. Also, have them paint any markings such as stripes or spots.

2. Students can then begin to consider what decorative, three-dimensional objects could be used for details. Could thin twigs be used for whiskers? Yarn for fur? Feathers? Pipe cleaners?

3. Set the masks aside to dry.

Session 4

1. Have students place the finishing touches on their masks using all the collected decorations (felt, fabric, fur, feathers, pipe cleaners, etc.) to make the masks truly come alive.

2. As the masks are set aside to dry, display them carefully. Have the class walk around looking at each other's masks, guessing the animals and appreciating each other's creativity.

Adaptation of Mask Making for Lower Functioning Students

For students with severe disabilities, you can still use the idea of the paper plate and handle. However, if holding the mask in place is a problem, punching holes on either side of the mask and running a string or rubber band through them will allow you to put the mask on the child's face for the final display of the artwork. To simplify the artistic process, you can eliminate the taping of the three-dimensional objects and the gauze. Instead, after mapping out in pencil where the features will go, have students use paint or torn tissue paper, construction paper, felt, or any other light but colorful material to create ears and facial features for the masks. It may also facilitate the process if your students all make the same kind of mask so that the shape of features and their placement can be done at the same time with the entire class. Students' masks will be light and colorful. This simpler process can be done in one or two sessions.

Follow Up: Using Masks

1. After the masks are finished, students may individually hold up their masks and assume the identities of their animals. They can create a special voice for their animal characters. The "animals" can have a discussion, in large or small groups: "What is happening to our home in the rainforest?" "What is happening to our food supply?" Ask the students how they feel about the answers to these questions. If you do not use the rainforest idea, students can make up a skit using animal characters and act out parts using the masks to help them "become" those animals.

2. After the masks have been actively used, they may be displayed on a wall or bulletin board.

3. An extension of the rainforest animal masks would be to create a mural (using paint, torn colored tissue paper, objects from nature, etc.) of the rainforest environment. Be sure to include sky, earth, water, and plant life—all the places where the animals would live. Animal masks could be a decorative border to the rainforest mural, or each "animal" could find where it would live in the mural. A slit could be cut in the mural in a tree, under a rock, etc., and the handles of some masks could be slipped into the slit so that only the animals' heads appear in their rainforest environment.

4. With storytelling, masks can be made or used to represent animals or other characters from folktales or fairytales. The story can be told by a narrator and silently acted out by the masked characters, or the masked characters can act out the story with planned or improvised dialogue.

5. In role playing, masks can be used to act out conflicts and resolutions in imaginary (or real) scenarios between friends or family. This can be more fun (and less threatening) than discussing interpersonal problems.

Visual Arts Glossary

Balance. The equal distribution of visual "weight" on either side of a center point.

Color. Has three properties:

> **Hue.** The name of the color

> **Value.** The lightness or darkness of a specific color

> **Intensity.** The brightness of the color.

> The three primary colors are red, yellow and blue. By mixing these in various combinations, green, orange, purple, and other colors can be created.

Drawing. A visual image created by a line. There are two basic kinds of drawings:

> **Contour drawing.** A detailed outline of the precise features of the visual model or subject.

> **Gesture drawing.** A drawing in which an action is captured and is more important than the exact space of the image itself.

Form. Another term for shape when referring to a visual image. Also refers to the overall composition or organization of all the visual elements in a work of art.

Line. A visual form, made usually by a pointed drawing or painting tool, that has an easily perceivable length but a width so small that it gives the visual impression of having only one dimension. Lines can embody qualities of energy or emotion. They can be smooth, jagged, straight, or curving or enclose a space to create a shape.

Pattern. A series or sequence of visual images that repeat over and over.

Rhythm. Usually associated with music, rhythm in visual arts relates to the quality of recurring patterns or images that allow a viewer's eye to move easily and quickly from one element to the next.

Shape. An area created by lines that enclose it. Or, an area defined by color masses whose outer edges determine the boundaries.

Texture. An element in visual arts that refers to the surface quality of an object as it would be perceived by touch, but in actuality it is perceived visually.

Unity. A congruity or cohesive quality among the elements of a design that implies a visual connection that was deliberately created.

Visual Arts Bibliography

Carlson, Laurie. *ECOART (Earth Friendly Arts and Crafts Experiences for 3–9 Year Olds)*. A Williamson KIDS CAN! Book. Charlotte, Vt.: Williamson Publishing, 1993.

———. *Kids Create! (Arts and Crafts Experiences for 3–9 Year Olds)*. A Williamson KIDS CAN! Book. Charlotte, Vt.: Williamson Publishing, 1993.

Dondiego, Barbara L. *Year Round Crafts for Kids*. Blue Ridge, Summit, Pa.: TAB Books and McGraw-Hill, , 1988.

Lauer, David A. *Design Basics*. College of Alameda (Alameda, CA). New York: Holt, Rinehart & Winston, 1979.

Similansky, Sara, Judith Hagan, and Helen Lewis. *Clay in the Classroom*. New York: Teachers College Press, 1988.

Terzian, Alexandra. *The Kids Multicultural Art Book (Arts and Crafts Experiences from Around the World)*. A. Williamson KIDS CAN! Book. Charlotte, Vt.: Williamson Publishing, 1993.

Treinen, Sara Jane, ed. *Better Homes and Gardens Incredibly Awesome Crafts for Kids*. Des Moines, Iowa: Meredith Corporation, 1992.

Warren, Bernie, ed. *Using the Creative Arts in Therapy (A Practical Introduction)*. New York: Routledge, 1993.

Visual Arts Music Appendix

The music listed here was drawn from a variety of genres, and most are instrumental pieces that may not be familiar to you. Even so, be sure to keep your own running list of children's songs and music that you come across to use in your arts activities.

Much of the music in the list can also be used for dance, drama, or music activities and should be referred to for these purposes. If there is no catalog number or the numbers have changed, ask for the music by the author's name and the title of the work. However, the majority of this music, especially the jazz and music from the Western European tradition (classical, baroque, romantic, etc.) is rather quiet and gentle in nature, to help create a harmonious atmosphere conducive to visual arts activities.

 Jazz

Artist	Title	Label	Catalog Number
Terence Blanchard	*The Billie Holiday Songbook*	Columbia	CK 5779
John Coltrane	*Ballads*	Impulse	
Miles Davis	*Kind of Blue*	Columbia	CK 40579
Curtis Fuller	*Blues-ette*	Savoy Jazz	SV 0127
Stan Getz/ Kenny Barron	*People Time*	Verve	314-510-823
Coleman Hawkins	*In a Mellow Tone*	Original Jazz Classics	6001
Joe Henderson	*Lush Life*	Verve	314-511-779
Milt Jackson	*Reverence and Compassion*	Qwest/Reprise	45204-2
Steve Nelson	*Full Nelson*	Sunnyside	SSC 1044D
Marcus Roberts	*If I Could Be with You*	Novus	63149-2
Jimmy Scott	*All The Way*	Sire/Warner Bros./ Blue Horizon	26955

 Classical, Baroque, Romantic (Western European Tradition)

Composer	Piece
Tommaso Albinoni	*Adagio in G Minor*
Johann Sebastian Bach	*Complete Lute Suites*
Johann Sebastian Bach	*The 6 Unaccompanied Cello Suites*
Samuel Barber	*Adagio for Strings*
Johannes Brahms	*Ballads*, op. 10
Frederic Chopin	*The Nocturnes* (solo piano)
Sainte Colombe	*Concerts A Deux Violes Esgales*
Johann Pachelbel	*Canon in D Major*
Erik Satie	*Gymopedie* no. 1, no. 2, no. 3
Erik Satie	*Gnossienne* nos. 1-6
Peter Ilitch Tchaikovsky	*Waltz Serenade*
Antonio Vivaldi	*The Four Seasons*

Group	Title	Label	Catalog Number
Anonymous 4	*An English Ladymass*	Harmonia Mundi	HMU 90708

	Title	Label	Catalog Number
	Faire, Sweet & Cruel (Elizabethan Songs)	Hogman/Lindberg (voice/lute)	B15-CD-257

New Age

Artist	Title	Label	Catalog Number
Doc Lew Childre	*Heart Zones*	Planetary Productions	
Malcolm Dalglish	*Jogging the Memory*	Windham Hill	WD-1046
Tangerine Dream	*The Collection*	Castle	CCSCD161
Enya	*Shepherd Moons*	Reprise	26775
Kitaro	*The Light of the Spirit*	Geffen	24163
Kitaro	*Dream*	Geffen	24477
Stevan Pasero	*Seasons*	Sugo	SR9253
Raphael	*Music to Disappear In*	Hearts of Space	HS11005
Ira Stein	*Carousel*	Narada MD	G1033
Liz Story	*Solid Colors*	Windham Hill	WD-1023
Andreas Vollenweider	*Down to the Moon*	CBS	MK42255

World Music

Artist	Title	Label	Catalog Number
Babatunde Olatunji	*Drums of Passion: The Invocation*	Rykodisc	RCD 20128
Bauls	*India: Initiation Songs of the Bauls of Bengal*	Buda Musique	92608
Hariprasad/ Zakir Hussain	*Venu*	Rykodisc	RCD 20128
The Gyuto Monks	*Freedom Chants*	Rykodisc	RCD 2011
Ella Jenkins	*African American Folk Rhythms*	Folkways/ Smithsonian	45003
Rossy	*One Eye on the Future One Eye on the Past*	Shanachie	64046
The Tahitian Choir	*Rapa ITI*	Triloka	7192
Glen Velez	*Doctrine of Signatures*	CMP	5445183
Zap Mama	*Adventures in Afropea 1*	Luaka Bop/ Warner Bros.	45183
Various Artists	*The Big Bang*	Ellipsis	3400
Various Artists	*Global Meditation*	Ellipsis	3210
Various Artists	*The Best of World Music Vol. 1, Vol. 2*	Rhino	71203, 21204
Various Artists	*African Songs and Rhythms for Children*	Folkways/ Smithsonian	45011

Folk

Artist	Title	Label	Catalog Number
Patrick Ball	*Celtic Harp from a Distant Time*	Fortuna	17011
Malcolm Dalglish/ Grey Larsen	*Banish Misfortune*	June Appal	JA0016D
Bob Kindler	*Tiger's Paw*	Global Pacific	79334
Madeline MacNeil	*Heart's Ease* T	urquoise	TRCD 5068
John McCutcheon	*Water from Another Time*	Rounder	11555
Loreena McKennitt	*The Mask and Mirror*	Warner Bros.	45420
Walt Michael & Co	*Step Stone*	Flying Fish	FF 70480
Simple Gifts	*A Place Just Right*	Purple Finch	PFP103
No Strings Attached	*Take Five*	Turquoise	TRCD 5060
Various Artists	*Celtic Odyssey*	Narada	ND 63912

 Native American

Artist	Title	Label	Catalog Number
Fernando Cellicion	*The Traditional Indian Flute*	Indian Sounds	5060
R. Carlos Nakai	*Canyon Trilogy*	Canyon	CR 610
R. Carlos Nakai	*Earth Spirit*	Canyon	CR 612
R. Carlos Nakai	*Desert Dance*	Celestial Harmonies	13033
R. Carlos Nakai + Peter Kater	*Honorable Sky*	Silver Wave	SD 507
Paul Winter + Friends	*Living Music Collection*	Living Music	LM 0008
Paul Winter + Friends	*Canyon*	Living Music	LM 0006

 Minimalism (Repetitive, Cyclical Themes)

Composer	Piece	Label	Catalog Number
Philip Glass	*Two Pages, Contrary Motion, String Quartets #2, 3, 4, 5*		
Steve Reich	*Early Works, Come Out*/1966, *Piano Phase*/1967, *Clapping Music*/1972,	Elektra/Nonesuch	79169
	It's Gonna Rain/1965	Elektra/Nonesuch	79169
Steve Reich	*Sextet*/1985, *Six Marimbas*/1973–1986, *The Desert Music*	Elektra/Nonesuch	79138

Instrumental Music with Animals as a Theme or with Animal Sounds

Artist	Title	Label	Catalog Number
Tom Chapin Group	*Mother Earth*	Sony Wonder	57678
Paul Winter	*Earth Voices of a Planet*	Living Music	LC 0019
Paul Winter	*Wolf Eyes*	Living Music	LM 0018
Paul Winter + Paul Haller	*Whales Alive*	Living Music	LM 0013
Various Artists	*The Animal Express*	MCA	10290

Composer	Piece
Sergei Prokofiev	*Peter & The Wolf* op. 67
Camille Saint-Säens	*Carnival of the Animals*

Index

About the Author

Paula Chan Bing received her bachelor's degree in music education from the University of Maryland and a master's degree in flute performance from Indiana University. She has performed with many orchestras and chamber groups throughout New York, including the Dance Theatre of Harlem and the Chinese Music Ensemble of New York. In the Broadway show *Miss Saigon* she played Western and Asian flutes, and has recorded many CDs, documentaries, and feature films, such as *Malcolm X*. With storyteller and author Margaret Wolfson, she has toured Europe, Asia, Sweden, and Australia, creating sound design for stories on world flute, percussion, and folk harp.

Paula has worked as an artist/educator for the Kennedy Center, the Los Angeles Music Center, and the Lincoln Center Institute, and presented at a creative arts conference in Gothenburg, Sweden. She is a music education specialist and artist trainer for the Midori and Friends Foundation and was director of education for the Queens Symphony Orchestra. At the Juilliard School, she is on the faculty of the Music Advancement Program and was associate director for Juilliard's first CD-ROM, which won two Codie awards in 1996 for "best innovative use of sound and music in a software program" and "best middle school educational music software program." In 2002 she was director of the Literacy through Jazz Institute, funded by the Dodge Foundation and the New Jersey Chamber Music Society and gives curriculum presentations for the education department of Jazz at Lincoln Center. For 10 years, Paula worked for Artsgenesis with special needs students and educators, training teachers in music and multiple intelligences theory. She dedicates her work on this book to her brother with schizophrenia and her mother and is very grateful to both Arts Horizons and Artsgenesis for the opportunity to create this handbook.

Courtesy of Paula Bing.